CONFETTI MOMENTS

52 Vignettes to Spark Conversation, Connect Deeply & Celebrate the Ordinary

AMY JAMROG

Printed in the United States of America

Published by Ethos Collective™
PO Box 43, Powell, OH 43065
www.ethoscollective.vip

LCCN: 2022917408
Paperback ISBN: 978-1-63680-098-1
Hardcover ISBN: 978-1-63680-099-8
e-book ISBN: 978-1-63680-100-1

Available in paperback, hardcover, e-book, and audiobook

Amy Jamrog is a registered representative of and offers securities, investment advisory and financial planning services through MML Investors Services LLC, Member SIPC. Supervisory Office: 330 Whitney Ave., Suite 600; Holyoke, MA 01040. The Jamrog Group is not a subsidiary or affiliate of MML Investors Services, LLC or its affiliated companies.

DEDICATION

This book is dedicated to all my loyal *Wednesday Wisdom* blog readers.

For more than two years, you enthusiastically responded to my weekly stories and shared that my words mattered to you. You were also the people who boldly suggested that this collection be packaged into a book. That turned out to be very good advice.

I will never forget that this project started with you.

CONTENTS

FOREWORD

Amy has thought long and hard about the daily dragons we all meet.

Often, those dragons are invisible.

What do people think of us, our choice of vocations, our politics, and our romantic partners? Do they think that in each case we are doing the right thing, the acceptable thing? Amy confronts these invisible struggles head-on by sharing her experiences, and with examples and insight shows us how to slay them.

Sometimes the challenges she brings to light are achingly personal, which makes the suggestions for how to deal with them both relevant and meaningful.

How do we say goodbye to our kindergartener at the bus stop on their first day of school? Or for that matter, how do we manage it thirteen years later after we have helped that same child, now a first-year college student, lug their trunk up three flights of stairs and the time comes, once again, to say goodbye?

Amy also shows us how to use memories of our early years to help others pursue their goals. She wasn't always the head of her own financial planning firm. In the beginning, as she shares, she took risks, built a business, and learned from her mistakes along the way. What's special about what Amy does in *Confetti Moments* is that she reminds us to enjoy our successes, but also to look back at our fledgling days—and then share those recollections with those who are just starting out. Those newbies often need a spiritual boost, and a tale of success through perseverance may be just the ticket.

Amy asks us to also consider the dragons we sometimes create ourselves. Have we ever broken a commitment? Promised more than we could deliver? It can happen to the most cautious. Was it a serious mistake? Perhaps. But, of course, it wasn't the end of the world. Still, it can gnaw at a person. Amy shows us how to consider it and still get on with our lives, armed with a new resolution or two.

Each short chapter, or Confetti Moment, is a new opportunity to reflect. In one of those Moments, she discusses the death of her father at age fifty, what he accomplished in his short life, and what he did for Amy, her sister, and her mother. She links the theme of life's uncertainty with that of a life well-lived and asks us to consider the quality of ours.

As befits Amy's career as a financial planner, many of her Confetti Moments involve the subject money.

However, in each Moment, she advises us to use money to go beyond materialism. She urges us to probe deeper, wider—to take steps that, in many cases, could be life-changing.

She encourages us to think thoughts that are positive, generous, and even forgiving.

Not only of others, but of ourselves.

Confetti Moments is that rare book that is both wise and supportive while also being entertaining and easy to read. And at the heart of every chapter is her assumption, present but never stated, that this is it—the only chance we have—to get it right.

Austin Kenefick
Retired Journalist
(and ninety-year-old uncle of the author)

GETTING STARTED

Years ago, my son was at a sleepover at his friend Dylan's house along with a dozen teenage boys. The following morning, I sat in the driveway, waiting to pick him up.

The front door opened, and I expected to see Charlie. Instead, it was Dylan's mom who emerged. She walked over to my car in her pajamas and slippers.

I panicked, wondering what she was about to say.

"Please excuse the outfit. I wanted to be sure I got to you before your son comes out."

I waited. She continued, "I want you to know what a great kid you have. Late last night, the boys ordered pizza and wings and completely took over my kitchen. When they were done, they headed to the basement to watch a movie and left their mess behind. But your son stayed and helped clear all the plates and cups from the table and loaded them into my dishwasher. I was so impressed! And I thought, as a mom, you'd want to know that."

Surprised by her words, I felt overwhelmingly proud. Since I anticipated a troubling report, her compliment landed unexpectedly. I knew instantly: This is a confetti moment.

A "confetti moment" is an experience of joy, surprise, or celebration. Sometimes, it's personal and not an event an outsider might care about. Other times, it can be a shared experience. A confetti moment doesn't have to be grand, like a graduation or a wedding. It happens during the times when we're celebrating the ordinary, and suddenly you think: *Cue the confetti . . . something terrific is happening to me right now.*

That's how Dylan's mom made me feel that morning in her driveway. I had been struggling as a parent of a fifteen-year-old boy, wondering if any of the advice or lessons I was trying to teach my son were ever going to sink in. And then she shared that little moment and made my day.

Welcome to *Confetti Moments.* This is a collection of stories meant to spark conversation, help you connect deeply with others, and celebrate the ordinary things in life.

* * *

I have been a financial advisor for the last twenty-five years, working with all kinds of families, business owners, and retirees. One thing is common among all of them: They have a deep desire to connect with others. Don't we all want to make a difference, not only in our own lives but also in the lives of others? And don't we also want to make the most of the time we have?

Sometimes we need direction—and encouragement. Every once in a while, it helps to have a little YOLO (you only live once) inspiration from an outside source to spark more moments of surprise and celebration.

Confetti Moments is that source.

Each of these fifty-two vignettes is written to pull you into a personal story. After you read each chapter, you'll be given prompts. The prompts will offer ways to make meaningful changes in your life *during the next week*. You can even use *Confetti Moments* like a journal and write your answers and reflections right here in this book. Some readers don't want to stop after reading one vignette. They want to keep on reading. If that's you, feel free!

Once you see how positively these stories impact you, I hope you'll be encouraged to share them with others. That's the whole point: to spark conversations and connect deeply.

No matter how you choose to use this book, know that each story is written to make you *feel something*. The subjects are about **being human** and **being humble**.

The best part?

Confetti Moments is easy. You just read, reflect, and let the prompts guide you. In this book, I give you fifty-two opportunities to practice having great conversations and making deeper connections. This book will show you how to take notice of and celebrate the ordinary things in our lives.

Cue the confetti! Let's get our fifty-two-week journey started.

CHAPTER 1

KIMCHI & EGGS

On Monday, I woke up feeling great. I was excited to start a new month, and I was ready to take on a busy work week. I got up early, poured my coffee, and decided I would go into the office instead of working from home. That meant I had to pack food, do a little extra prep, and get dressed for business (i.e., no house slippers).

First, I went to the kitchen to pack a hearty salad for lunch. Then I sautéed egg whites, spinach, and kimchi for my breakfast and put the mixture into a to-go container. I wanted to get to the office early, have my breakfast while there, and get a jump-start on emails before I had to show up for the first meeting of the week with my whole team.

I was feeling energized and motivated as I prepped for the day ahead. As I thought about the clients I would be meeting with this week, I began brainstorming ideas for them. I got dressed in a fancier-than-normal outfit. If I was going to truly take on the day, I was going all out.

That's when I noticed my Louis Vuitton briefcase tucked in the corner of my closet. I hadn't used it since the pandemic started. It had been sitting collecting dust for almost two years. My bags, along with my high heels, went unused for too long. Today was the day to change that. I thought: *I love that bag! I worked hard to buy those shoes! Today I'm going to put them both to good use.*

Packed and ready to conquer the week, I got into my car, turned on my favorite country station, and headed to work. Even though my commute is only eight minutes, I wanted to take time to crank up some great jams and keep my already-awesome day on the right track. It was 7:20 a.m.

Halfway through my ride, I was about to make a right-hand turn when the car in front of me stopped quickly. I slammed on my brakes. In two seconds, I heard my briefcase fall off the backseat, hit the back of the driver's seat, and slam to the floor behind me.

I tried to reach it but could not. From the noise it made when it hit the floor mat, I knew my entire container of colored pencils I use for journaling had spilled everywhere. I should have known better than to carry them in an open cup, but it's easy to access them all day for my notes if they aren't in a less accessible travel bag.

No big deal, I thought. I can pick up pencils, reorganize my briefcase, and keep my positive mojo going.

I was just about to turn into my parking lot when I noticed a really disgusting smell. It was like rotten eggs mixed with garbage, and I worried it might be coming from my car.

And then the smell became oddly familiar.

Kimchi and eggs: my breakfast.

I had put my food in a to-go container that had seemed safe for travel. But apparently, when I stopped quick and my bag tipped over, the lid to my container came undone. My entire breakfast was now loose in the bottom of my Louis Vuitton briefcase.

I parked my car, got out of the front seat, and reluctantly opened the door to the backseat.

There were my fifty colored pencils all over the floor, points broken off.

Yet that was nothing compared to the scrambled-egg-and-kimchi breakfast now soaking into the bottom of my Louis Vuitton briefcase.

If you are not familiar with kimchi, it's a healthy probiotic—but it's made with fermented cabbage, ginger, and garlic.

It tastes good but smells disgusting.

In fact, the only reason I thought it was okay to bring such a foul-smelling breakfast to work was the fact that I'd be there early and have it consumed before my team arrived.

My early-to-work Monday plan was derailed by my having to deal with this unexpected mess. And it had to be dealt with ASAP.

At first, I wasn't sure what type of cleaner to use. I went upstairs to see if there was anything mild. All I found under the kitchen sink were Clorox bleach wipes. Probably not suited for Louis Vuitton leather. Ugh.

I went back downstairs to check the supply closet and only found wet Swiffer refills. I trekked back upstairs to the kitchen and settled on some Dawn for dishes and warm water.

Suddenly I also regretted the high heels I was in after several flights of up-and-down stairs.

All I could do was laugh. A lot.

Picture me in my office building, all dressed up and alone, sharpening broken pencils one at a time at my electric pencil sharpener while simultaneously trying to stuff my designer bag with paper towels, attempting to remove the fermented cabbage stench from the bottom of it.

Need I say more? You can see the whole scene, can't you?

That's when I humbly was reminded that **sometimes the plan is not the plan**. We can be prepared and organized and ready for every appointment on our calendar yet end up unexpectedly sidetracked. Or with a breakfast-filled briefcase.

Remember this story when you find yourself having a disappointing or derailed kind of day. These are the moments when we must choose to take life a little less seriously.

Instead of getting upset, give yourself a break, share your story with someone else, and, when all else fails, you're welcome to take a moment and laugh at mine.

Ideas to Spark, Connect & Create this week:

- Is there an upcoming event or important meeting you have, and you are doing everything imaginable to make sure it's perfect? Step back and take a moment to make space for the unexpected. What could possibly go wrong? Actually, ask yourself this question and build in some provisions and safety nets as a proactive measure.

- Think back on a time when a plan didn't go as you had hoped. Are you still reliving that experience in your head, like a recurring nightmare? Jot down any small elements from that event that you could give yourself credit for. **Find some redeeming qualities within the disaster**.

- Continue thinking about that time when your plans did not go well. What were the lessons learned from it? If you can see past your upset, anger, and embarrassment, what could you now say in hindsight that you took from this experience?

- Most importantly, forgive yourself. What's done is done. You found some highlights, you learned some lessons—now give yourself permission to move on.

Notes and Thoughts

CHAPTER 2

LESS, BUT BETTER

Like most Friday nights, we planned on watching a show before going to bed. We didn't have anything specific in mind, and we had about an hour before our normal bedtime. We clicked on Netflix.

"What are you thinking? Do you want to watch something funny? Or something more serious? Maybe we could check out that documentary on the college admission scandal? Or start the final season of Ozark . . . wait, that's on Hulu . . . what about something easier like the Great British Baking Show?"

This back-and-forth dialogue went on and on as I scrolled through, quite literally, hundreds of Netflix choices.

You probably won't be surprised that twenty-five minutes later, we were still trying to choose a show. And the hour we once had available had dwindled to half. Scrolling aimlessly through program choices had wasted thirty minutes of our life.

How often have you found yourself unintentionally wasting time? Or spending time doing something without much meaning, significance, or impact? What if you were to step back and take an honest inventory of the way you spend each of the twenty-four hours you have in a day? How many "unconscious choices" do you make? If you suddenly got intentional about your time, what might you do differently?

I have been working on this **time inventory project** for several months now, inspired after reading the book *Essentialism* by Greg McKeown. He explains if you want to be an "essentialist," you need to look at all the ways your time gets spent.[1]

You then need to ask yourself over and over the important question: "Is this task/project/choice essential? Will doing this make my life happier and more fulfilled?" If the answer is no, then an essentialist would choose to no longer do it.

Many of us wish we had more time in the day yet still opt to do things that provide little satisfaction. Social media, TikTok, getting sucked into the evening news— we go down this path almost aimlessly, only to find that our choices do not enhance our lives at all. By doing less, having less, and even worrying less—we could certainly free up time.

I spoke with my friend Robyn about this. She packs lunches for her three kids every morning before they leave for school. Robyn has been repeating this task for years. Yet she recently became frustrated because the kids have started to change their minds about what they want to eat. They argue and bicker. Robyn feels underappreciated. This negative interaction sets the day off on the wrong foot for the whole family. The kids complain about what's in their lunchboxes, they leave no time to make adjustments before their bus shows up, and inevitably food comes back at the end of the day uneaten and often wasted.

Robyn started asking herself what an essentialist would do.

Without any explanation to her children, she changed the routine. She laid out all the lunch options on the counter for the kids to assemble themselves. Between the sandwich fixings, the Cup-a-Soup choices, and various chopped-up fruits and veggies in Ziploc baggies, there were plenty of things from which the kids could choose.

You won't be surprised to hear **that they loved picking different items personally each day** from the selections on the counter. The whole prep process took less time for Robyn. The new routine became more fulfilling for the kids. The arguing and bickering stopped altogether. Robyn turned something annoying into something positive.

In *Essentialism*, McKeown explains that an essentialist does *less but better*. "You can do *anything*, but you don't have to do *everything*."[2]

As he explains, a non-essentialist is always adding more to his or her plate. But an essentialist is constantly eliminating unnecessary or dissatisfying things in an effort to simplify life.

What if *less* could be *better*?

Ideas to Spark, Connect & Create this week:

- If you took inventory of all the things you do each day, what on your list are you declaring no longer essential?
- What would you like to start eliminating? By when?
- With that freed-up space and time on your calendar, what would you choose to do instead?

Notes and Thoughts

CHAPTER 3

BUY THE DAMN TRUCK

I got the email confirming that my clients had sold their medical practice, and the proceeds from the sale had been officially deposited into their account. Dr. Marion had cared for his patients for thirty-five years. His wife had been his office manager. This was the event they had been working toward for years.

In preparation for this moment and as their financial advisor, I had updated their plan and reviewed their retirement income needs. Dr. Marion knew exactly how the money from the sale of the company was going to be invested. Despite this clarity, they both wanted to hop on a Zoom call.

Turns out, they were *really nervous* about retiring.

Dr. Marion had been an aggressive investor since the day I met him, but suddenly he was becoming concerned about volatility. They both had dreamed of the day when they could be 100 percent retired, but now they wondered what the heck they were going to do on Monday when the practice was no longer theirs to run.

We set up a call to talk through all of it.

In that conversation, I walked them through the entire plan again. Dr. Marion nodded in agreement as I reminded him about each recommendation I had made. His wife kept looking at him, wondering if my reassurance was making her husband feel any more secure.

After an hour, we had discussed just about everything related to their money—the stock market, their investment allocation, and their income needs—which would all be met with the wealth they had accumulated.

Yet Dr. Marion was reluctant.

He asked, "Is there anything else I'm supposed to be doing?"

I answered, "Yes. Before the year is over, I want you to take time to celebrate. *Retiring is a big deal.* You have worked hard for almost four decades to build a valuable practice. You successfully sold your business for exactly the amount you hoped to be paid. What you have accomplished is extraordinary. I think you need to do something special for yourself."

Dr. Marion smiled and turned to his wife. "I hadn't really thought about celebrating. I was just trying to get through the sale and be sure it was official. Maybe this is the perfect time to finally open that bottle of Caymus we've been saving."

"That's a start . . . " I replied. "How about thinking a little bigger than a bottle of wine?"

Mrs. Marion and I were on the same page. She smiled and reached for her husband's hand. "Why don't we go look at new trucks this weekend? Yours has 200,000 miles on it. I think it's time."

I agreed with her and encouraged the idea. "Have you seen the new F150s? They are beautiful! The technology is awesome. Why don't you go online and look them up?"

Dr. Marion already knew exactly what I was referring to. He confessed he had already built several versions of his dream truck online over the past few months.

Immediately he started sharing all the details of the new King Ranch versus the Lariat. He was so excited about the features, colors, and technology available in the new models!

Without hesitation, his wife commented, "John, you deserve it! You've waited so long to get to this moment. We can afford it. You love it. Do me a favor and buy the damn truck!"

Then they turned to each other and kissed. He squeezed her hand, pretended he wasn't getting choked up, and promised he'd go looking at trucks that weekend. They were both happy and relieved by the time we ended the call.

While it may sound like a funny thing, **sometimes we need permission to celebrate**. We are trained to save and save and save for the future. Yet when we finally get there, we often have a hard time making the transition from accumulating money to spending it.

Even though he had sold his business for millions of dollars, and the truck had a sticker price of $80K, it became my job to assure Dr. Marion that it was affordable and acceptable for him to make the purchase.

When he questioned my encouragement and asked, "But isn't this money for retirement?" I had to remind him:

This is retirement.

As a financial advisor, it's a privilege when I get to congratulate a client on their successful journey and provide continued guidance as they transition to the next phase in life. Often my advice is more about encouraging people to spend and assuring them they can afford the new purchase or the celebratory vacation.

Next time you're talking with a friend or a family member, and you know they have something worth celebrating, remind them to take action. Encourage them. You know it, and I know it, but sometimes they may not realize that it's okay to buy the damn truck!

Ideas to Spark, Connect & Create this week:

- Have you recently reached a big milestone in your life, or do you have one coming up? What did you do, or will you do, to commemorate your accomplishment?
- Who in your life is going to be reaching an important milestone this year? A big birthday, a retirement, or maybe even paying the last college tuition payment? What can you do to help them celebrate?
- Thinking back, is there an accomplishment that you (or someone close to you) achieved but had no fanfare and no official acknowledgment of it? Reminder: It is never too late to celebrate! What could you do to bring some celebration to that important moment, even if it happens to be after the fact?

Notes and Thoughts

CHAPTER 4

NO PLAN B

I was interviewing for the position of financial advisor. It was 1996. I was excited as well as nervous, and I felt prepared for the questions the group was going to ask me.

I didn't know it at the time, but I was about to get the best advice of my career—and I hadn't even started it yet.

The recruiter for the firm asked me what I enjoyed about the job I was currently working in. I was in health insurance with a local insurance carrier, and I shared all the things I liked about my account manager position. She took some notes. The manager then asked why I was considering leaving a salaried position with a corporate credit card and company-issued Ford Taurus for a job that was going to be 100 percent commission with no fringe benefits.

Great question.

I explained I considered myself a risk-taker, that I wanted to control my income, and that I wanted to be rewarded for my hard work. I also shared that I wanted to be self-employed and answer to no one but myself. It also seemed that if I became a financial advisor, I would have an impact on people, help them with their money decisions, and create long-term relationships. I had a hunch these were the right buzzwords to use, but they also rang true for me.

The sixty-two-year-old advisor who was also in our meeting (and someone who would eventually end up being my mentor) had been quiet up to that point. Then he turned to me and asked, "And if this financial advisor job doesn't work out for you, what's your backup plan?"

Without pause, I responded confidently: "I know I can always go back to my corporate job. In fact, my company would probably even hire me back if this didn't work out."

"WRONG ANSWER!" he belted out. I jumped a little in my chair.

He continued, "If you have a backup plan, you'll never be 100 percent committed to making this work out. You'll always have one foot out the door. **If you want to succeed, you need to give up your Plan B**."

The idea made me nervous.

He continued to explain: "If you're willing to throw away the idea of a backup plan and commit wholeheartedly to this career, I will invest in you. I promise to teach you everything I know. I believe that with my experience and your enthusiasm, we could do incredible and very meaningful work together. Think about it. It's a big decision."

I didn't need to think about it. **I just knew it felt right**.

At that moment, I believed everything he was saying. And I believed even more in the opportunity in front of me—to be coached and trained by one of the best advisors in the business and to begin a career dedicated to helping others get what they wanted in their lives. That sounded fantastic to me.

I bravely spoke up.

"I don't need to think about it anymore. No backup plan, just this. I'm totally in." I put my hand out to shake his.

That was it. My career as a financial advisor began.

As I look back on that meeting now, more than twenty-five years ago, the advice I received was **critical** to my success: **No backup plan**.

Was it risky to commit 100 percent? Sure.

But it worked out—for me, for my clients, and for my family—100 percent. I love this work.

What about you? Do you have one foot committed to something and one foot simultaneously pointing toward your Plan B if this doesn't work out for you?

You might have a backup plan for your current career.

You might have a backup plan for your marriage.

Either way, having one foot in and one foot out **never equals commitment**.

What would it mean to throw away your backup plan and instead commit 100 percent to the thing that's right in front of you?

Committing wholeheartedly could:

- End up resulting in a phenomenal career.
- Result in a fantastic marriage.
- Make possible anything you set your wholehearted self to accomplish.

Ideas to Spark, Connect & Create this week:

- Is there a Plan B you have been secretly holding onto? What would it take to give it up?
- If you had no fear and you knew it would all work out, what would you put 100 percent commitment into?
- What **will you commit to this week** to get you moving in a better direction?

Notes and Thoughts

CHAPTER 5

COMPARED TO WHAT?

I got up early to ride my Peloton before work. It was 6:30 a.m., and I chose a ride with a great '80s playlist to wake me up and kickstart my morning.

If you have a Peloton bike, you know that every ride begins with a warm-up. I scanned the Leaderboard to see who was riding with me. There was no one listed on the leaderboard I recognized. But I noticed there was a male in his fifties riding in front of me on the screen. I start pedaling harder and faster to try to catch him. I didn't know him, but he was the same age as me, and I am extremely competitive. I looked at the number he had next to his name that tracks his output, and I saw that my number was two points lower than his. Given my drive to win, I increased my resistance. Over the next minute, I passed him. I instantly felt victorious. Mind you, I was only five minutes into the thirty-minute ride, but I was pretty sure I was crushing it.

As I passed him, he sent me a high-five. This is a thing unique to Peloton: by pressing a little high-five button next to someone's name, you can send them a pop-up icon that gives them a little high-five, essentially telling them they're doing a great job. It seems silly, but it *really* works. It feels like instant congratulations and a message of encouragement from a virtual stranger. If you have ridden a Peloton bike or treadmill before, you know exactly what I am describing. People high-five you, and you high-five them back, and this can sometimes go on for the entire workout. You generally don't know any of the people you're sending these congrats to. The most fascinating part—at least to me—is that it doesn't matter. It's part of the culture, and the encouragement is constant. It's one of the things that keeps riders coming back.

Halfway through the ride, I was sweating, singing out loud to the '80s music playing full blast from my speaker in the basement, and trying to follow what the instructor was telling us to do. I noticed that I was getting closer to my PR—that's my personal record, which the computer tracks in every ride. As soon as I saw that I could potentially beat my record, I started pedaling faster. Meanwhile, another guy sends me a high-five as he cruises past me and skyrockets to the front of the pack. He was moving so quickly up the leaderboard that no one could catch him. I found myself yelling out loud and cheering for him (alone in my basement, mind you), and I sent him another high-five. The guy was a machine and his power was impressive.

Eventually, my ride came to an end. My heart rate was high, and my water bottle was empty. I ended up finishing toward the middle of the pack, with many people surpassing me in the final minute as I slowed down. I had beaten my own personal record. It was only 7:00 a.m., and I had a new PR to kick off my day. I was elated! Exhausted physically but mentally elated.

Then something occurred to me.

If I had solely compared myself to the other riders, my ride would have been disappointing. Middle of the pack. Fiftieth percentile. Mediocre. Meh.

Instead, I compared that ride to the other thirty-minute rides I had done before. I was proud to see that I had done better that day than ever before. Sure, I looked to the other riders for encouragement to pedal harder. I high-fived their efforts, and they high-fived mine. At times I was ahead of some of the people while simultaneously lagging behind others. Regardless, I was doing my own personal best.

Isn't this a great way to go through life?

What if, instead of constantly comparing ourselves to others to see how we measure up, we compare ourselves **to ourselves**?

How often do you find yourself comparing your efforts to other people and ending up disappointed? Ever think that sometimes it might be more productive to compare yourself to your own "personal record" in whatever it is you are tackling? Ask yourself, "How am I doing compared to *me at my best*?" rather than, "How am I doing compared to a random person who seems to be outpacing me?"

I'm not saying that there's anything wrong with a little competition. After all, it's competition and the desire to improve that has been the catalyst for so many people to advance, grow, get better, and experience incredible breakthroughs in life.

As you're competing—whether it's on the bike, in school, or at your job—don't forget to send friendly high-fives along the way. Some days, you'll be at the front of the pack. Other days, you'll be lagging as others outpace you. Let all of these experiences help push you forward. Keep focusing on where you are going, and take a moment to appreciate where you happen to be *right now*.

Ideas to Spark, Connect & Create this week:

- Think about the last time you were competing and lost. Who were you competing against? Was this a reasonable "race" where you were comparing yourself to an actual competitor? As you look back on this, was it healthy or unhealthy competition?
- Who's the person you constantly compare yourself to? Is it time to let this go?

- When was the last time you competed and won? Was the focus solely on you, or did you take time to high-five others along the journey?
- Who could you reach out to and congratulate them on a job well done, even if it's after the fact?

Notes and Thoughts

CHAPTER 6

SOMETIMES WE NEED A WIDER LENS

In addition to my financial planning practice, I also coach hundreds of financial advisors across the country. Last week, I sent a survey asking each of my coaching clients for feedback to help me improve their experience in working with me.

A surprisingly high number of people responded. The results were incredibly positive. On the 1–10 scale of happiness and satisfaction, the average score was 9.5—excellent! People's comments were very complimentary. Many added additional notes thanking me for going above and beyond to help them problem-solve or coach them through a challenging issue. Overwhelmingly, they said they got value from our work together, they found the deliverables useful, and they were **very likely** to refer others to the program.

All this sounds positive, right?

I would have been . . . except for the one person who gave an overall score of four. The respondent said they felt "okay" about my program, that the deliverables were "okay," and that they "might" refer others to me in the future.

Despite the stats from other respondents whose scores were nines and tens—and the glowing reviews from the rest of the people who answered the survey—I immediately zoomed into the one person who gave me the less-than-stellar review. I wanted to call the person and get more feedback, apologize for whatever was missing in my process, and see what I could do to fix or improve their experience.

The person about whom I was obsessing opted to remain anonymous in the survey. Therefore, calling them was not a possibility because I could not pinpoint exactly who they were.

Instead, I obsessively replayed conversations in my mind and tried to recall any indication of dissatisfaction from any of my participants over the past few weeks. Words like "okay" and "fine" and "maybe" did not settle well with me. This negative feedback from one dissatisfied person became all I could think about.

That is when I realized that my **zooming in** and focusing solely on one mediocre score completely discredited the other positive scores I received. I became blind to the compliments and kudos because I could not see beyond the one seemingly negative response.

How often do we zoom into a negative detail and obsess over it—completely losing sight of the bigger picture?

Have you ever had a night out at a dinner party, conversed for hours, felt like you had a great time—but then returned home only to rethink one comment you made that you wish you hadn't spoken? And you continued to replay that conversation over and over, cringing at those few words you wish you could take back? Before you know it, the dinner you had perceived as fun just one hour before becomes a lousy memory, ruined by something you are now recalling as being negative. You **zoomed in** on one tiny detail and let it overshadow all the positive parts of the night.

Our friends went with their kids to Disney recently. They planned an epic trip and tried to pack in everything possible into five days. On the last day of their vacation, their six-year-old twins had a complete meltdown midday at Animal Kingdom. Understandably, the family cut their time short at the park and instead returned to the hotel. After a nap, the kids spent the afternoon lounging by the hotel pool, which included a water slide and a lazy river ride. When I later asked how the trip was, my friend said it may have been a mistake to take the kids to Disney at such a young age. She was still zooming in on every negative detail of the Animal Kingdom meltdown.

But if you ask the twins how their vacation was, they'll tell you without hesitation that it was "super awesome," and they'll enthusiastically share a dozen highlights—including how much they loved their last day at the hotel pool.

Often, kids know better than grown-ups how to **use a wider lens to focus on the bigger picture**.

What about you? Have you ever looked back on your holiday season and reminisced about how much joy your family experienced, or did you focus instead on the Visa bill you received in January, regretting how much money you spent on gifts?

Do you reminisce about your amazing trip to Italy and all the decadent meals and wine you tasted? Or do you obsess about the five pounds you gained there and regret the daily pizza you enjoyed so much?

Are you someone who zooms in and focuses on a single, negative, overshadowing detail, letting it ruin the bigger picture and all the otherwise great memories associated with it?

Me too.

We could all use some practice **living life through a wider lens**.

I thought about this a lot as I went back to those survey results. It took some real effort on my part to become more open-minded. Only when I was finally able to zoom out was I able to feel proud of the bigger picture.

The next time you look back on a scene, an experience, or a conversation, and you start to gravitate toward one negative detail, instead try to apply a wider lens to your perspective. Focus on the macro rather than the micro. Zoom out rather than zooming in.

This wider perspective can make all the difference.

Ideas to Spark, Connect & Create this week:

- Think back to a time when you zoomed into a negative detail and lost perspective on the bigger picture. Maybe it was a conversation with a friend or loved one, and it did not go as planned. Is there someone you need to apologize to? It does not matter how long ago it happened—**an apology is never too late**.
- Is there an area in your life where you tend to zoom in? Maybe it happens when it comes to politics or parenting or your boss's leadership style. What if you committed to changing that response right now? The next time it comes up, you'll be prepared to approach it with a wider lens. Watch the difference it makes—for you *and* for others—just by having that new awareness.

Notes and Thoughts

CHAPTER 7

KEEP THE CHANGE

My sister Nicki and I had made a promise to each other more than thirty years ago: We vowed that for the rest of our lives, no matter where we were or how inconvenient it might be at that moment, we would *always* stop at a child's lemonade stand. We also agreed to tip the young entrepreneurs generously.

Nicki and I grew up in a quiet neighborhood and not near a main road. Setting up a lemonade stand, and working at it for hours in the summertime, was a big commitment, and it took patience to wait for the customers to show up.

In our experience, we learned there were several important elements in creating a successful lemonade stand.

- First, we needed lots of ice. The lemonade— seemingly the star of the show—didn't even have to be *that* good if we added plenty of ice to each cup. Customers always seemed more excited about a refreshingly cold drink on a hot day than they were about their lemonade actually tasting good.

- Second, we needed a big and colorful sign. Lucky for us, our mom was artistic and always had extra cardboard and Magic Markers on hand. She would draw bold bubble letters for our sign, and we would fill them in with bright colors. We firmly believed our advertising attracted more people.

- Third, we knew from experience that it was best to set up shop at the end of the workday and catch neighbors on their drive home. If it was hot, our sign's message was clear, and we offered a refreshing beverage. Who'd pass that up?

- Last, the real leverage was to *not* have a lot of change in our money box. That's because not having change for customers made it easier for them to leave us a tip. When we'd open the cash box and there weren't many coins in there, the customers would often say, "Keep the change." (You might think this to be a sneaky tactic, but at ages nine and seven, we thought we were quite clever.)

The profit we would make from our lemonade stands became our Cape Cod spending money at the end of the summer. We had goals to make a lot of money because we had plans for all the souvenirs and things we would buy on our vacation. It didn't take long for us to realize that if people were stopping for lemonade, they might buy other things too. We eventually added Rice Krispies Treats, Toll House cookies, and anything else Mom helped us bake. These additional offerings ultimately helped boost our profits.

And when I say "profit," I am referring to the money we got to keep *only after paying back Mom* for all the supplies we needed. I didn't know back then, but our parents taught us lifelong lessons by loaning us money for lemons, sugar, and cups, then tallying up the expenses and making sure we paid back the microloan at the end of the day.

Nicki and I learned how to calculate how many cups of lemonade we had to sell before we'd break even. Although she might say I was bossy, I thought we were a good team. Studies have shown that the activities you loved doing as a six- or seven-year-old child often shape and influence who you later become in life. Not surprisingly, Nicki ended up being a math teacher, and I became a financial advisor.

I loved every aspect of a lemonade stand as a kid. It taught me basic business skills, marketing strategies, and even how to leverage. That is why I'm still committed to helping any budding entrepreneur in the lemonade-stand space.

I encourage you to join my sister and me in our promise to never drive by a child's lemonade stand without stopping, purchasing a cup, and letting the kids *always* keep the change.

Ideas to Spark, Connect & Create this week:

- Is there a young person in your life you could teach these important lessons to? What if you found out their passion, helped them develop and market their product or talent, and taught them basic business skills in the process?
- Did you rock a lemonade stand as a child? Is that skill on your résumé? What if you showcased your entrepreneurial history and business acumen in your résumé, video intro, cover letter, or in the actual interview by sharing the story of your lemonade stand success? This simple action could help you stand out among all the other candidates vying for the job.
- Are you currently doing a job you love? If not, think back to what you enjoyed doing when you were six or seven years old. Does it spark any career change ideas for you? Don't judge or think about how this could ever happen. Simply write down the ideas you are thinking about. Take time this week to daydream about these new possibilities.

Notes and Thoughts

CHAPTER 8

CRAFTERDAY

Saturdays have been renamed Crafterday in my house. My nine-year-old niece BB and I get together periodically on Saturday mornings to work on fun projects. I set up a craft table for us in my basement, and all my art supplies are spread out and ready for her 9:00 a.m. arrival. BB takes her time each week sorting through the crayons, glue sticks, and colored pencils, choosing exactly the items she's interested in for the week's project.

In early February, we spent three hours cutting out hearts from colored scrap paper and gluing them into collages to make homemade valentines. For someone so young, BB is incredibly focused, relaxed, and interested. Remarkably, so am I when we are engaged in these creative activities. Typically, I'm not one to sit quietly for very long. But on Crafterday, I find myself completely immersed in the project, and time passes by for both of us.

Crafterday also includes music. I've started sharing old songs I love with BB. She gives me a thumbs-up or thumbs-down. If it's a thumbs-up, we add the song to our "Crafterday Jams" playlist. Can I tell you how happy it makes me that she has learned to appreciate Duran Duran, Earth, Wind & Fire, and The Go-Go's? Picture the two of us sitting side-by-side, singing out loud, carefully cutting out tiny hearts, and making valentines until it's time for lunch.

My sister often joins us for lunch after Crafterday and then takes BB home. For some reason, we had no interest in ending our day of fun, so I opened a 500-piece jigsaw puzzle I had gotten for Christmas. I spread out the pieces on the dining room table. "Let's just get the edges started," I suggested. BB enthusiastically sorted puzzle pieces into piles of colors, then each of us took a corner, and before we knew it, it was 4:30 p.m. when the last piece of our puzzle snapped into place. When all was said and done, we spent **seven hours that day** doing nothing but creative, relaxing, fun, crafty things. And, of course, also singing, "We Got the Beat." It was a perfect day. I was reminded of the simpler things in life: relaxation, play, and *fun*. Who doesn't love that?

At the end of **your** busy week, I highly recommend testing out your own version of Crafterday. When was the last time you opened up a brand-new box of Crayola Crayons©, smelled that unmistakable waxiness of a fresh box, and colored? Maybe you're someone who'd love to go down to your workshop to do some woodworking or dust off an easel to do some painting. Recently my mom took out her old sewing machine and started doing some simple sewing projects.

Many of us are so time driven. We live by the clock and are in a perpetual rush to finish something just so that we can move on to the next item on our to-do list. What if you took out Crayons and colored simply for the sake of coloring? What if you dedicated the afternoon to work on a jigsaw puzzle, and paired it with a playlist of nostalgic songs from your childhood?

What's the thing you'd do "if only you had the extra time"?

Make the decision that **now's the time**. And when your project is done, don't forget to thank yourself for the opportunity to stir up those old creative juices!

Ideas to Spark, Connect & Create this week:

- Is there a craft you've always wanted to try? An indoor project you'd love to take on during the winter months? Or an outdoor project you'd love to do in the nicer weather?
- Think back to when you were a kid. What did you do back then that had you lose total track of time? Was it playing with friends? Riding your bike? Roller-skating? What if you bought yourself

a jump rope, picked up a harmonica, or spent an hour cutting out snowflakes from paper? Whichever activity you choose, pick something that will allow you to reconnect to the joys of being a child.

Notes and Thoughts

CHAPTER 9

NEVER HIT THE SNOOZE BUTTON

Years ago, I worked with a great coach who was an expert in teaching people skills for following through. For a long time, I had been frustrated that despite my good intentions and inspirational goal setting, I'd found myself not finishing what I had started. I hired Coach Pete to help me with this challenge. When Pete and I started working together, he shared a story of his client Jeff who had a problem with not being able to get up in the morning to work out—even though it was an important goal of Jeff's.

After asking Jeff a few questions, Pete discovered that Jeff didn't have a problem working out. Instead, **his problem was with his snooze button.** The guy had great intentions to get up at 5:45 a.m. And he knew that all it took was getting out of bed, physically putting his feet on the floor, and heading to the bathroom to put his workout clothes on. But the one obstacle that existed between his bed and his workout was his snooze button.

And so it would go every day: The alarm would buzz at 5:45 a.m., Jeff would "want" to get up, and he would justify that nine more minutes of sleep would still give him enough time to work out. He'd hit the snooze button.

Nine minutes later, he'd do it again and again and again until the nine minutes turned into thirty-six minutes. Then Jeff had no choice but to get up for work. And by then, there simply wasn't enough time for his workout.

Day after day, Jeff would struggle with this same pattern. Pete, being a follow-through expert, helped his client see that this pattern had to be changed. And it wasn't about having more willpower, trying harder, or making Jeff feel bad for not being able to overcome the allure of the snooze button. It was much simpler than that.

Pete asked Jeff to make one small tweak. The same 5:45 a.m. alarm remained on his nightstand. But Pete asked Jeff to also set a second alarm clock, this one for 5:47 a.m., **in his newborn baby's room**. When the 5:45 a.m. alarm sounded in his room, Jeff had 120 seconds to jump out of bed and run down the hall to the baby's room before the second alarm woke her. That was it. Even though the snooze button was still an option, the second alarm down the hall proved to be more motivating to get Jeff up without hesitation. No one in the house wanted to wake the baby that early. Problem solved!

What about you? How often do you set goals, intend to follow through on them, and for whatever good—or even justifiable—reasons, you fail to accomplish them? Think about your New Year's resolutions. How are those going? (Do you remember what they were?) If you find yourself frustrated or disappointed by your lack of follow-through, maybe you need more triggers to remind your brain that you are switching up your old patterns and doing things differently from now on.

Most of us are not wired to follow through without a lot of additional prompts to stay focused. If this sounds like you, maybe it's time to change your patterns and processes and inform your brain that things are about to change! Following through is not easy, but if we can set up our world with reminders everywhere, we can improve the likelihood of hitting our most important goals.

Ideas to Spark, Connect & Create this week:

What small changes are you going to make to build reminders into your day? Try some of these:

- Change your password on your devices to reflect something important to you: ItalyVacationNext Year, 20LBSdown, or workoutsmakemehappy! Every time you log into your devices, you will have to think about this new password. When the password becomes routine, change it up again.

- Wear a watch? Move it to your other wrist. Will this be uncomfortable and different? You bet. **That's the point**. As soon as you get used to your watch on the other hand, move it again. Your job is to constantly remind your brain that things are not the same anymore.
- Set alarms on your phone at different parts of the day to remind yourself to eat healthily, get up from sitting, or pick up the phone to call your mom.
- Change the background picture on your phone, your iPad, **and** your laptop. Put a picture of your next vacation destination on there or a physical reminder of something you are going for. If you want to lose fifteen pounds before the summer, put the word fifteen **everywhere**.

Notes and Thoughts

CHAPTER 10

SARA'S FAVORITE SUNSET

Tim and Sara have been clients for almost twenty years. Their three kids were young when we first began our work together. Our early meetings were focused on talking about their dreams for their future, writing down their goals, and creating a plan to ideally have them retire early. They have always been hardworking, smart, and motivated. They knew when the kids were young that they wanted to provide them with the same kind of educational opportunities they both had.

Over the years, I helped them reallocate their 401(k) plans at work, apply for life insurance, and set up college accounts in the state where they lived.

As the years went on, Tim and Sara saved more for college, sold their house, upgraded to a nicer home in a more affluent town, and continued to advance in their careers. When they could afford to, they increased their 401(k) contributions, paid down their home equity loan, and started building an investment portfolio for a rainy-day fund.

The kids grew up. Their firstborn was ready for college, and the money to pay for the tuition was saved in her college account. The same happened for their second child, followed by their youngest. By systematically investing in the three college accounts, Tim and Sara had saved enough money to pay for twelve years of tuition (minus the $10K in student loans they wanted each child to have responsibility for). **They had so much to be proud of.**

More importantly, they had accomplished all of this without compromising their own retirement. Sure, they took vacations here and there, occasionally upgraded their vehicles when necessary, and made the expected repairs to their home. But the whole time, they remained focused on retiring at sixty-two, paying down their mortgage, and living debt-free in their retirement years.

My favorite thing about Tim and Sara was that **they were always coachable**: they trusted my professional opinion and followed the advice I had given them in their financial planning meetings each year.

At the beginning of this year, we met for a Goals & Priorities Review. The market had been great the year before, and I wanted to rebalance their accounts and make sure their retirement plan was still on track.

Sara kicked off the conversation by announcing, "We have some news to share that might come as a surprise to you." I panicked for a moment, not sure if the news was going to be good or bad. Tim saw the look on my face and chimed in.

"It's all good! You know we have always loved the beach. And we've dreamed of one day having a home closer to the water in our retirement. But we weren't planning on this for another ten years."

I could see where this was going.

"There is a particular street alongside the beach not too far from where we live now. We often drive down on quiet evenings and walk there because it happens to be where Sara swears are the best sunsets in the world."

Sara interjected with so much enthusiasm, "You know how sometimes you say, 'The plan is not the plan'? Well, I had told Tim years ago that I had no intention of moving and that my thinking has always been to stay in our house long-term and retire there. But the *one exception* was a house on that beach that I fell in love with the first time I saw it. It's the most perfect location and would give me access to my favorite sunsets every single night. I said to Tim that if it ever comes up for sale, we must buy it!"

Guess what came up for sale?

In the most perfectly orchestrated story, Tim and Sara's dream house suddenly got listed in November. The sellers were older and ready to downsize. They wanted one last Christmas at the beach and asked for a February closing. The timing for many potential buyers would have been too far out, but for Tim and Sara, it was perfect. It gave them one final Christmas in their own home, then ample time to pack, stage, and list their house for sale.

They made an offer on their DREAM HOUSE. And although they were not the only ones bidding, for some reason, the sellers chose them.

In a matter of one weekend, Tim and Sara's offer was accepted on the beach house, and their own home sold after a bidding war. The math on both transactions worked beautifully. The sellers got what they wanted at exactly the time it made sense for them, and Tim and Sara were going to be getting a house they had dreamed of—but never imagined would be possible so early in life.

They moved into their new home the week of Tim's birthday—only in their mid-fifties. The transition could not have gone more smoothly.

Six weeks later, they were settled in, their family photos were hung on the walls, and new couches had just been delivered. They were so proud, so excited, and still feeling a bit of disbelief at how beautifully it all came together. As Sara shared, "I would never have thought that my favorite sunset could be right here, in front of our house, for us to enjoy and appreciate every single evening for the rest of our lives."

To me, Tim and Sara's story conveys several important lessons.

First, they remind us that **saving systematically for future goals actually works**. The earlier you start, and the more you save, the more flexibility you will have later in life—especially if you want to make small or big changes to your plan!

The second lesson is that **focus and determination pay off**. Tim and Sara's willingness to be coachable, to stick with a monthly savings plan, and year after year to keep doing whatever it took to educate their kids, pay off debt, and invest for retirement **all paid off**.

If this family reminds you of yourself, congratulations. You are clearly on the right path!

On the other hand, if you're reading this and struggling to relate to these people because you're feeling like you're lacking focus—maybe even wondering why your own future isn't as clear to you as theirs was to them—then I urge you to use Tim and Sara as your motivator and catalyst.

While it is great to start planning early, keep in mind that it is also never too late to start.

Ideas to Spark, Connect & Create this week:

- Do you have a vision for your future? Start by brainstorming where you might like to be over the next three years. New job? New home? New city? Start making your list. Then start to expand your thinking to ten years, twenty-five years. Think big! And write down everything that comes to mind. (And when you get to the final chapter of this book, just know that we'll be coming back to this important topic!)

- Do you have a money savings plan? If not, you might want to work with a financial advisor—someone who can help you think about your vision for your future and then map out an action plan to help get you there.

Notes and Thoughts

CHAPTER 11

MODERN-DAY SHIPWRECK

In 2021, a 220,000-ton vessel named *Ever Given* got stuck in the Suez Canal. It is still somewhat unclear whether it was a sandstorm, an unexpectedly high tide, or human error that caused this gigantic boat to wedge its way into the outer banks of the canal. According to Richard Meade, the editor-in-chief of *Lloyd's List*, the issue could be simply summarized: "This is a very big ship. This is a very big problem."

He wasn't exaggerating.

The stuck cargo ship caused a tremendous waterway traffic jam. It was said to have held up $10 billion in trade each day until it was finally released the following week. But the 1,300-foot cargo ship (carrying nearly 20,000 containers) needed a salvage team to calculate complicated questions regarding engineering, physics, meteorology, and earth science to free it.

According to *The New York Times*, "If the tugboats, dredgers, and pumps were unable to get the job done, they would have been joined by a head-spinning array of specialized vessels and machines requiring perhaps hundreds of workers: small tankers to siphon off the ship's fuel, the tallest cranes in the world to unload containers one by one and, if no cranes are tall enough or near enough, heavy-duty helicopters that can pick up containers of up to twenty tons—though no one has said where the cargo would go."[3]

To a layperson like me, it seemed from the online photos that it was an easy physics push-pull problem to solve. What was unclear, however, was how deeply wedged into the sand the ship was, making it impossible to maneuver it without the help of diggers, tugboats, and the rising tides.

When the sun and moon are in alignment—as was the case with the full moon that week—their combined gravitational pull results in exceptionally high tides. On Sunday, water levels rose eighteen inches above normal in the Suez. This presented a very tight window that the crews had to work within: Each time the tide rose, the 220,000-ton vessel stood a better chance of becoming buoyant. But it needed dozens and dozens of tugboats to help with the rescue. Together they were able to use tidal forces to help free the ship. By early afternoon they had succeeded, with the ship once again fully afloat.

Last year, it was said that 18,840 ships made it through the canal without an accident. Unfortunately for the crew aboard the *Ever Given*, that mishap caused a global backup of hundreds of cargo ships and forced many of them to "take the long way around" (which cost up to $26,000 more in fuel per day per ship).

The traffic jam was so epic it could be seen from satellites in space!

I know this story is dramatic, and its impact was felt across the world in terms of trade, cargo, and cost. But the more I read about this story, the more I cannot help but think about the captain and the crew: **How were they feeling that week**?

What if it turns out that the mess was caused by a small human error on their part? When the final investigation is complete, will we learn that they were the ones to blame for this colossal cluster?

Have you ever made a mistake and found that it totally snowballed beyond anything you could have imagined? Have you ever felt like the captain of the *Ever Given*, where your slight miscalculation may have led to a complete disaster?

I think about a friend of mine who had the creative foresight to bring a huge community together for a one-hour inspirational webinar in the middle of the pandemic. She pulled strings to get a very famous keynote speaker booked for her event. Guests were so excited about the opportunity. Turns out that 1,000 people paid the registration fee and logged in for the Tuesday presentation.

She knew this was going to be a life-changing moment in her consulting career—and could even put her on the map as a thought leader and curator of great online content.

She had tested her technology, confirmed and reconfirmed her guests, and was beyond thrilled when hundreds and hundreds of people started entering the Zoom room.

The only person not on the call was the keynote speaker.

That's when she suddenly realized—obviously too late—that she had confirmed him for Wednesday instead of Tuesday. Her webinar instantly became a complete—well—shipwreck.

If this has ever been you—when you've managed to miscalculate just enough to wedge your own proverbial cargo ship into the canal bank and get completely stuck—can you cut yourself some slack?

We all make mistakes, some albeit larger than others. Sometimes we must be humble and ask for help. Sometimes we simply need to give ourselves the grace to forgive and move on.

More importantly, if you have ever witnessed this happen to someone you know, maybe one of your employees, a friend, or even a stranger, **did you do anything to help them**?

Did you watch from afar and comment what a mess they had gotten themselves into but offer nothing in terms of support?

Or were you similar to the excavators and tugboats who each did their small part to collectively pitch in and help fix the disaster with a coordinated group effort?

Next time you witness a colossal cluster—whether it is your fault or someone else's—give grace. Remember, we are all human, and we certainly have all made mistakes. And then do what you can to quickly mobilize your resources, pitch in, and help avert the crisis.

Ideas to Spark, Connect & Create this week:

- Think back to a time when you made a huge mistake—something that caused a real problem for you or for someone else. Does it still weigh on you? Do you need to take a moment this week to forgive yourself one final time and move on? Write it down.
- Think back to a time when someone else in your world made a mistake—big or small—and you **did not** help them out. Even if this memory seems like old news to you, consider that the person who made the mistake might still be feeling lousy about it. Take time this week to reach out to them, acknowledge the situation, and apologize for not helping them at that moment. Own up to your lack of leadership and offer your sincerest apology.

Notes and Thoughts

CHAPTER 12

YOU CAN'T TAKE IT WITH YOU

One of the projects I committed to recently was cleaning up my online photos. I had almost 10,000 pictures on my iPhone, which were taking up too much space. I scrolled all the way back to 2005. That's where I found almost 400 vacation pictures from our first family trip to Disney. Every amusement park ride, every costume-wearing character, several plates of yummy food—you name it, I had taken multiple pictures of all of it. To be able to snap photos from a phone was amazing back then. In one device, you had a phone, a watch, an alarm, and a camera. And to have all your photos at your fingertips—easy to share and post and reflect on—**was and still is incredible**.

It was a treat to scroll through blasts from the past, one year after the next. The places we had been, the people we'd spent time with, several relatives who are no longer with us…all captured one frame at a time. The clean-up project was a joy to complete.

In the end, I managed to decrease my photo count down to about 6,500. Still a ton of pictures and many years' worth of memories. There were also plenty of pictures that I didn't need anymore—hundreds of action shots from kids' sports, flowers I had grown in the yard, and so many sunsets. It was easy to delete many. But some I simply couldn't part with.

This exercise got me thinking about technology and the past. I remember when I was younger, having to buy rolls of film and then sealing up the finished roll in a yellow pouch and sending it to Kodak for processing. Remember that? You'd also have the option to check off on the envelope whether you wanted "singles" or "doubles," all the while not knowing what photos you were getting, if the pictures were going to be blurry, off center, or terrific. There was no preview. Then you'd wait *for weeks* for the prints to arrive. How many times did you get prints of your thumb or a totally fuzzy, indiscernible scene? Even better, you may have paid for doubles of that shot!

I still have many of those prints in old photo albums, along with the brown negative strips. But my mom has the most impressive collection of actual printed photos. Over the years, she's accumulated box after box after box of prints (still in envelopes, with the negatives), as well as Polaroids and black-and-whites. Some were hers, and some had once belonged to my grandmother.

Mom would periodically ask questions like:

"Should I do something with all these pictures?"

"What am I saving these for?"

"Do you think anyone cares about these besides me?"

During her early years of retirement, Mom had plenty of time at home to focus on house projects. She started to sort through hundreds and hundreds of her photos. She broke them into categories, separated people into different families, and thoughtfully asked herself who might care about these memories. It was quite an undertaking. Some of the pictures evoked wonderful memories—others were painful and sad when she reminisced about how many of our loved ones had passed.

In the end, Mom did something special: She created little care packages of pictures for many members of our family. Many people, myself included, received an unexpected package in the mail filled with a collection of memories that Mom had curated for each of us.

Mom found the answers to her earlier questions: First, there was no need to save all the photos for herself. And yes, people *did* care about them. In fact, many of my aunts and uncles commented that some of the photos they received were pictures that they didn't know still existed—**or had never even seen before**.

Each person was so appreciative of the gift and the thoughtfulness that went into it. Sure, Mom could have scanned the photos, archived them online, and sent a Google album to everyone. But what was more meaningful was having the paper photo in hand, like in the old days.

My mother's generous and creative project reminded all of us that **you can't take it with you**. All those photos could have sat in boxes for another twenty years until someone else inevitably would have been tasked with having to figure out what to do with them.

Consider this: What if you decided to give some of your things away now instead of waiting for someone else to inherit them after you've passed?

For years I have had conversations with friends and family about their collectibles and other precious items they have been hanging onto. Inspired by my mom's idea, I have helped people figure out how to turn their collectibles into meaningful gifts within their lifetime.

I'd like to share a few to spark some inspiration:

- Helen had gotten too frail to live at home and was moving into an assisted living facility. She would no longer have the space in her new apartment for her traditional Christmas tree. During her packing and sorting, she took all her precious Christmas ornaments and divided them into three separate collections—one for each of her children. She surprised them on Thanksgiving with a package for each, and the timing was perfect as it was right before the start of everyone's holiday decorating. Her children and grandchildren cherished the memories associated with each unique piece as they decorated their own trees that year.

- After George lost his wife, Jean, he was left with a lifetime of memories—many of which could be found in Jean's jewelry box. Earrings, rings, brooches, and many other gifts he had given her over the years were piled up in that box and no longer used by anyone. George took her collection to a local jeweler and had many of the old pieces remade into five necklaces and gave them to his two daughters and three granddaughters. Each necklace was new to them but was made from something recycled and special from Jean.

- Bill did not have much to give his son and daughter-in-law in terms of money. He simply lived on his pension and social security. But he did have a collection of antique guns in his basement safe. He no longer used them, and his son was never interested in them. Bill contacted an antique gun buyer who came to his house, safely assessed each piece, offered Bill a lump sum check, and safely took them all away. Bill received more money than he could have ever imagined for the collection. He used that money to add to a Roth IRA for his son and to open a college account for his ten-year-old grandson as well.

Think about the things that are meaningful to you. Maybe this could prompt a conversation between you and your parents or grandparents. Or perhaps you want to give your children their "future inheritance" today when it might be more meaningful to them rather than when you are gone. And how wonderful might it be for you to have the joy of seeing that impact on others in your lifetime?

Ideas to Spark, Connect & Create this week:

- Do you have collectibles that are valuable and that might be special to share with loved ones during your lifetime?
- What if you invited your family or friends over and asked them to peruse your belongings to see if there is anything they might be interested in once you are no longer here? Consider giving that item to them for their birthday or at an upcoming Christmas instead of waiting until you are no longer alive for them to inherit it.
- Have you ever sat down to write a letter of intent to your loved ones? This is a letter that outlines all the wishes you have for the way your personal belongings get distributed once you have passed away. You can name specific people as the beneficiary of jewelry, meaningful collectibles, antique furniture, or your favorite old pickup truck. This is a way to make sure that your belongings are left to the people you intend. What's already coming to mind? Jot your ideas down right here:

Notes and Thoughts

CHAPTER 13

GOING ALL IN

It was Felix's sixth birthday celebration, and that is apparently what brought their family to Disney for vacation. I only knew this because I read it on the front of everyone's T-shirts. There were nine family members traveling together: Felix (the birthday boy), Carlos, Inez, Juan, Maria, and two sets of grandparents (Grammy, Grampy, Abuelo, and Abuela). They were all clearly Disney fans. In addition to their "Happy Birthday Felix" T-shirts with their own names printed on the back of each, they all wore coordinated black shorts, white sneakers, and white baseball hats. They stood in front of us on one of the rides at the Magic Kingdom, and I couldn't help but admire their total commitment to coordinated family outfits and the special celebration of Felix.

We saw them the next day at Epcot—all nine of them, this time in a different customized family T-shirt with the same full-commitment outfits.

When it came to planning for their special family vacation, whoever was in charge of managing all those details was **all in**. Felix and his family weren't the only ones. Throughout our four days at Disney, we saw dozens and dozens of families, newlyweds, and youth groups—each with matching T-shirts, some with personalized baseball caps, and many with years' worth of trading pins attached to their backpacks. These were dedicated Disney fans, **all in** for their trip.

This reminded me of the people who go all in for their trips to Tanglewood. Tanglewood is an outdoor concert venue in the Berkshires of Massachusetts. If you were to see the place when it's empty, it doesn't look like anything special. But on a concert night when James Taylor or the Boston Pops are playing, you'll see thousands of people sitting on blankets with the most elaborate picnics ever. In addition to fancy food platters and wine in decanters, many guests also pack linens, china, crystal, and even fresh flower arrangements for their tiny tables. Their commitment to the Tanglewood Experience is incredible. In fact, it's worth going just to see the spreads that people create. If you've been there, you know that the guests who participate are **all in**.

I have a friend with two pet chihuahuas. He also has a closet with more than 200 outfits for his dogs. This might not make sense to you, but when it comes to his dogs, Geoffrey is all in.

My neighbor has the most elaborate garden. Her floral boxes each contain the most gorgeous flowers, plants, and vegetables I've ever seen. She spends hours and hours every day tending to them with love and patience.

What about you? When was the last time **you were all in** for something? Maybe it's been a while. Is it time to reconnect to an old passion of yours?

Whatever it is that you decide to commit to, give it your all—and while you're at it, look around and begin to really appreciate others who are doing the same.

Ideas to Spark, Connect & Create this week:

- Is there a hobby you used to love but haven't done in a long time? Is it inspiring to think of reconnecting with it? In doing so, what if you went **all in on your commitment**?
- Is there a special occasion coming up? Maybe someone's milestone birthday, a big anniversary, or a special accomplishment to celebrate? What if you cooked them dinner, hosted a party, or did something special to commemorate it? And what if you went **all in**, paying attention to every little detail, to make the event or moment extra special for them?

Notes and Thoughts

CHAPTER 14

UN-COACHABLE

I have been a financial advisor for twenty-five years. I also coach financial advisors. Coaching started as my side hustle years ago and has since become some of my most meaningful and favorite work. I used to coach people one-on-one. Now I assemble cohorts of like-minded individuals and coach them in groups as a mini-community. The dynamic can be very powerful when the right people are put together with the right motivators. People who are coachable and ready for growth are my favorite people to be around.

Over the years, I have learned to charge a reasonable fee for my work. Whether someone pays a monthly subscription or I bill them an hourly rate, I am crystal clear that they pay me to deliver relevant content, create fresh ideas, and help propel them and their businesses forward.

What amazes me is how many people are willing to hire a coach, spend their hard-earned dollars on advice and guidance, and then choose to implement nothing, **not** grow, change **nothing**.

How does someone *pay a coach* and then *not be coachable*? I can tell you because I was one of those people.

It was back in 2002. I was returning to full-time work after having a baby the year before. I needed to get on track, increase my profitability in my practice, and be able to afford to pay my assistant as well as myself. I was told by trusted colleagues that it was time to hire an executive coach.

The idea was uncomfortable and rather expensive. I agreed to pay $1,200 a month to work one-on-one with an expert in my field. My goal was to increase my income by 30 percent within a year. If I increased my income by 30 percent, I thought, I could also justify the cost of the coach.

I got referred to a well-known coach in our industry. We met. He started by assessing my practice, my calendar, my production, and my pipeline. We met a few more times. He really understood me. He began to point out places where I could improve my outcomes. He was coaching other advisors with practices much more successful than mine, so I knew that what he was observing about my business was probably true. In our meetings, I would listen intently, agree with his assessments, write down great ideas, and commit to making changes—both big and small. I found him to be inspiring.

But then I'd get back to thinking about the stress of having to work more while also raising a baby. I'd obsess about upcoming appointments, having enough time to prep for them while also thinking about how to strategically look for new clients. Then I'd get sucked into my usual business-related insecurities and revert to old habits and what was familiar.

Essentially, I had changed nothing.

Three months into the coaching relationship (and after I paid the third bill), my coach said this: "I need to be direct with you. You are smart and talented, but you are a terrible client. You have made zero progress in our work together, and I think I should fire you."

Fire *me*? Why would he fire me when I was paying him to *help* me?

That's when he said something that will sound obvious to you but was a complete shock to me.

"Amy, I don't think you are aware of this, but you are not coachable."

Not coachable? How could someone **with a coach** not be **coachable**? It made no sense.

He proceeded to point out six ideas that he had recommended over the past three months and how **I had not followed through on a single one**. He showed me where my business metrics were off, where my calendar was still not time-blocked, and that I made no time for personal well-being—all things I had committed to improving. His coaching was clear and direct. I agreed with it all. But I had neither improved nor changed anything in ninety days.

I had spent $3,600 on a coach…only to learn I was not coachable.

To this day, I believe it was the best investment in myself I had ever made, mostly because, in that moment, I realized that **I didn't want to be an uncoachable person**. I wanted to change. I knew that being uncoachable was holding me back.

I asked my coach to give me another ninety days, and I promised I would do what he told me to do. The positive results were almost instant.

What was even more surprising was that I found it easier to be coachable than to resist. That was the game-changer.

I started to wonder if my being "not coachable" was true in other areas of my life. I recalled failed exercise and diet programs, the gym membership I enthusiastically paid for but didn't use, business books I bought and never read, and annoying habits I promised to work on in my personal relationships but kept perpetuating. I saw confirmation all over the place that I was not coachable.

I started to listen and take advice in other areas as well. I realized that if I wanted to grow and succeed in business, I needed to trust the experts who had come before me. I started being more willing to ask for help and turn to others to point me in the right direction and give me ongoing guidance.

The experience was humbling and enlightening. I started to believe the investment in coaches and outside professionals was an investment not just in me but also in my marriage, my family, and my overall happiness.

Fast-forward to today. I have had a coach, have been in a coaching program, or have participated in a study group of peers for the past twenty-plus years. The collective wisdom of these individuals—and what I continue to learn from them about myself—has been immeasurable.

The learning never ends. **Being coachable is humbling**. The ongoing investment in my personal and professional growth is something that has made all the difference—in all areas of my life.

What if today is the day you decide **you** are worth the investment?

Ideas to Spark, Connect & Create this week:

- Do you have a coach? Terrific. Take time this week to thank him or her for their dedication to your growth and success.
- Thinking about hiring a coach but have not taken the leap? Trust me: It's probably the right time.
- Resisting paying for a coach because you think it's too expensive? Ask yourself, "Too expensive compared to what?"

- Feel like you are coasting, plateauing, or not growing much these days? Ask yourself if you have become un-coachable. And then take the leap and hire a business coach, a personal trainer, a therapist—someone who could propel you forward and help get you unstuck!

Notes and Thoughts

CHAPTER 15

DECADENT, YET DESERVED

On Sunday, I did something highly unusual for me. I sat on my deck and read a book from start to finish.

For many of you, this would not be unusual at all. In fact, reading books might be what you do every weekend.

Not me.

I spend a significant amount of time every week—especially Sundays—writing my own material, blogging, and working on a new book. Rarely do I take the time to read someone else's book. But this week I did, thanks to a new friend. During a phone call, Courtney mentioned a book she thought I'd enjoy called *Heart Boss* by Regan Walsh. I told her I had never heard of it. A few days later, it arrived in my mailbox, thanks to her.

I know you're not supposed to judge a book by its cover, but I always do.

I opened the Amazon package and immediately noticed the bold graphics, the feel of the paper, and the catchy subtitle. On Sunday afternoon, I opened the front cover and started with the intro. The author's writing grabbed my attention. Her story felt like my story. It was one of those books I wished I had written for the world to read. I was hooked.

There I was on Sunday, sitting in an Adirondack chair, spending consecutive hours reading a book. No big deal, right? **For some reason, it felt decadent.** I loved it. I had no sense of the time, and it didn't matter.

The whole scene had me wondering, "Why don't I do this more often?"

Normally I do not read books until vacation. I save them until we go on a trip, pack them in my beach bag, and lie on a chair in the sunshine, day after day, losing myself in the pages and the stories. I love actual paperback books, not a Kindle, not audiobooks. I appreciate turning pages, dog-earing corners, and holding the physical book in my hands. Reading, it turns out, makes me happy.

But I had not taken a vacation in a while. And like you, I'm busy on weekends. Sitting down to read a book never comes up for me as a possibility. It occurred to me on Sunday, however, while in the middle of *Heart Boss,* how much I love to read. (Note to self: Read more. **Enjoy other people's words and stories.** Do not wait until vacation to enjoy this treat.)

Which leads me to this important question: What's your "Read a Book on a Sunday" equivalent? Is it taking a hike in the woods? Drawing? Fishing? If you unplugged and did something **totally decadent** for yourself, what would it be?

One friend makes gourmet cupcakes when she wants to do something special for herself (I've been the recipient of the cupcakes. Yum!).

Another friend goes into his woodworking shop in his basement and makes incredible, time-consuming, beautiful cigar humidors.

My son opts to take a ride in his car with no destination, cranks up his favorite music, and just drives.

In her book *Heart Boss*, Regan Walsh talks about being busy, overscheduled, and stressed. She points out how unrealistic it is to fantasize about having "more" time. The truth is, we all have the same twenty-four-hour days. **It is our choice how those hours get used**. We cannot conjure up more hours in the day to do the things we love. Instead, we must free up the hours we have, make different choices, and deliberately make stuff happen.[4]

What would you do if you had more time?

Ideas to Spark, Connect & Create this week:

- Over the next seven days, consider what you're going to do to unplug, relax, and do something decadent. Bake cupcakes? Go for a ride? Take in a movie all by yourself? Send a great book to a friend?

- Most importantly, how are you going to take back some of those prescheduled hours for yourself? What could you say no to, cancel, postpone— just to give yourself back some much-deserved time? This is a gift worth giving yourself. Haven't you earned it?

Notes and Thoughts

CHAPTER 16

DECISIONS, DECISIONS

I was talking with a friend who shared with me confidentially that she and her husband had recently made the decision not to have children. It took them years of thoughtful conversation together, as well as individual personal work, to come to this important conclusion. They love the life they have together—just the two of them—and don't want to change their dynamic. They also have meaningful careers they want to advance in. Not to mention that neither of them ever saw themselves as parents.

But my friend didn't know how she was going to explain this decision to others and was dreading the inevitable conversations.

When I asked why she felt she needed to justify this decision to anyone, with emotion, she shared her list of reasons: My in-laws are expecting grandchildren. My mom is hoping I have kids soon so they can grow up with my brother's kids and be similar in age. All my friends have kids. Having kids *has always been expected* of us, and I imagine our decision will be disappointing to many. I also worry that they'll think we are being selfish. I can already hear their advice:

- You don't know until you have children what a blessing they will be.
- We all felt that way at some point until we had our own kids, and it changed everything.
- No one is ever ready to have kids, but you two will figure it out.
- How can you have a fulfilling life without children?
- At some point, you will be older—who will take care of you?

I could feel my friend's pain.

I started thinking about the decisions we make, what and who we take into consideration when we make them, and how hard it can be to reach a final decision. Even then, with all our conviction mustered up, we still worry about what people will think of us and our choices.

Maybe you have a romantic relationship you want to end, but you aren't sure how to break the news to your family. Maybe you want to quit your great-paying job to reduce stress and live a simpler life—but you worry you won't be able to keep up financially with your friends anymore ... so you just keep working.

Is there a decision you are stuck trying to make? Are you worried about other people's opinions? Do you sometimes let other people's feedback carry more weight than you should?

I know I do.

I often struggle with people's feedback and perception. (Who doesn't?) I've considered others' opinions when I decided which college to go to, which career to choose, who I chose to marry the first time, the way I parent, the way I choose to spend money, the person I married the second time around, and the life that my wife, Kim, and I have created together—all of these decisions come with some low-grade insecurity about what people are thinking, as well as **what they are not saying to me** (but might be saying to each other when I'm not around).

This worry about what others think can really stop us from moving forward, making powerful choices for ourselves, and living a life we ultimately love—despite others' opinions.

Is there a decision you have been intending to make but are still waiting for the "right time" to commit to it? Worried about what your mom, your boss, or your friend will think?

Consider that the right time to make that choice is right now and that the only person's opinion that matters is yours.

Ideas to Spark, Connect & Create this week:

- Is there a place in your life where you are stuck in indecision? Simple as this advice might be, make a Pro and Con list. Write down every different option you are considering, then make the Pro and Con list for each decision you need to make. You'll be amazed at the clarity this exercise provides you.

- Often people come to us to share about a decision they are trying to make. Although they may present the options they're considering and the feelings they're feeling about each, **keep in mind they may not be looking for your feedback**. Before you launch into your opinion about how you think they should move forward, take a moment to pause and then ask then, "Do you need me to listen while you talk this out loud, or are you actually looking for my feedback?" It is a powerful question, shows empathy, and gives the person a moment to decide whether they want to know what your thoughts are. Sometimes when we share with a friend, we are looking for their support but not necessarily their opinion. Knowing the difference can really help in determining your ultimate outcome.

Notes and Thoughts

CHAPTER 17

LOWER YOUR EXPECTATIONS

Last fall, at a charity auction, I was the winner of a family portrait session. This was something I had been wanting to get for my mom for years. I was thrilled I won the package. Not only did it include a framed portrait, but it also included a trip to Portsmouth, New Hampshire, to the photography studio, along with an overnight stay at a nice hotel. I thought we could make a family adventure of it all.

Having been to that hotel before, I knew the trip was going to be great. The hotel sits along the water in a quaint New England town. The restaurants there are enjoyable and hip, and everything is within walking distance. Even the lobby bar is a trendy place to hang out.

I genuinely enjoyed the trip the last time I was there. I talked up the adventure with the family, told them about my favorite Mexican and BBQ restaurants, and rallied my mom, sister, niece, and son for an April road trip.

On a sunny Saturday, we piled into my sister Nicki's minivan. Everyone had their overnight bags packed. My partner, Kim, sent us on our way with a batch of homemade oatmeal cookies, as well as a couple bags of tortilla chips and salsa in case we needed any snacks.

The ride took three hours. The photo shoot took two more. So far, it was a total success.

Everyone was in great spirits as we headed to the hotel to check in and get some dinner. As we pulled into the parking lot, I asked my son, Charlie, to check the sign by the parking meter. "All good," he said, "Free parking . . . Saturday and Sunday." We parked, grabbed our belongings, and headed into the hotel lobby.

The last time I had been to this place, it was winter. The lobby then was toasty and quiet, with a fire burning in the big fireplace.

But on this trip in April, the place was noisy and jam-packed with people, including a bride and her sash-wearing bridesmaids. Turns out, there were not just one but two weddings happening at our hotel that weekend. I immediately felt disappointed by the loud and bustling vibe.

After checking into our rooms, I guided my hungry family next door to the delicious Mexican restaurant. Unfortunately, many of the wedding guests were already booked for a pre-party, and there was going to be zero availability for ninety minutes.

I quickly opened my Open Table app and found a reservation at a nearby BBQ restaurant. We walked four blocks. Online, the menu featured three pages of incredible meals, creative side dishes, and several seasonal salads. In person, however, we were each handed a piece of paper by the hostess. At the top of the page was the word "Menu," followed by a typed apology for their abbreviated meal choices, lack of kitchen staff, and an inadequate number of waitresses.

Instead of three pages of food, they had literally four items to choose from. There was no kids' menu. There were no side dishes, no vegetarian options, no vegetables, and—wait for it—no salads. The kitchen, according to the hostess, had forgotten to place a lettuce order. The only options were a plate of brisket, wings, or pulled pork egg rolls. And french fries.

Disappointed and now even hungrier, we opted to return to our hotel's rooftop restaurant for some better, healthier food. We retraced our steps four blocks back.

Unfortunately, the rooftop restaurant was so busy, there were no reservations for the rest of the night. The hostess suggested we go back downstairs to the lobby bar and order takeout from the rooftop—and they would gladly deliver it downstairs to us.

With minimal energy left, the five of us dragged our feet back to the elevator and headed to the lobby bar. The lobby was completely empty, and the bar had a "closed" sign handwritten on a piece of paper. I inquired at the front desk. They were very sorry to share that the bartender's grandfather had passed away unexpectedly, prompting her to leave early. The bar, they assured me, would reopen tomorrow at 7:00 p.m. **He apologized when he also informed us that we would not be able to sit there tonight**.

I was so disappointed. Not only was the place nothing like I had experienced the last time, but it was also nothing that I had promised my family. It was not at all what I had expected.

Defeated and still hungry, we decided to go up to our rooms, put on pajamas, and call it a night. That's when I remembered the oatmeal cookies and chips and salsa that Kim had packed "just in case." We divided the snacks among the five of us and made the best of it. I reminded everyone: At least our hotel has a top-notch breakfast buffet.

In the morning, we found out that there was only one waiter for the entire restaurant and that the breakfast buffet was apologetically "light" due to a significant staff shortage: no omelet bar, no bacon, and no chef specials like they usually have. Toast with coffee was the best we could hope for.

We decided to head home earlier than planned.

We packed up our few belongings from our respective rooms, checked out, and brought our bags to the car. That's when my niece spotted a $35 parking ticket on the windshield of Nicki's minivan. My son had read the meter too quickly. It actually said, "Free Parking during the week, **must pay** on Saturdays and Sundays."

I could not help but laugh. I understandably could have chosen to be angry, disappointed, and regret the trip altogether. (All those choices did cross my mind.)

Or I could be willing to pause, regroup, and simply lower my expectations. In the parking lot at that very moment, I put the $35 ticket in my purse and reset my expectations for the rest of the trip.

The ride home was filled with laughs and jokes about the hotel. The disappointing breakfast was overshadowed by a spontaneous stop at a Pizza Hut on the way home. We all enjoyed a gooey, delicious cheese pizza in the minivan. Then we made a stop at the Kittery Trading Post, and Nana bought everyone candy and treats. We cranked up fun songs and sang along together on the highway. Even the twenty-one-year-old got along with the nine-year-old all the way home.

Six weeks later, Mom's family portrait arrived in the mail just in time for Mother's Day. She commented not only about how much she loved the gift but also how much she loved our trip together. In her mind—despite the understaffed hotel and our hungry bellies—the experience was still special. My son agreed: "We should do that again sometime."

The next time you make a plan, and it doesn't go as expected, take a moment before you decide what to do next. How will you react? Be angry? Get annoyed at a restaurant for not having any salads? Or pause, take a deep breath, and adjust your expectations?

Keep in mind, this is not about lowering your *standards*—it's just about lowering your expectations at that moment.

Sometimes we must lower the bar to realize we can enjoy an experience, even if it doesn't live up to our original plan. With patience and perspective, we can all find gratitude and grace in any situation.

Ideas to Spark, Connect & Create this week:

- When was the last time you planned for something, and it did not go as expected? As you reflect on it, what was your reaction?
- Is there a way to look back on that experience and reframe it? What good came out of it? What lessons did you learn?
- Think about upcoming plans you have. Is there something you are excited about and looking forward to? What are your expectations for that event? Are there any unanticipated things that could happen? Brainstorm what could go wrong and be prepared for them.
- If something goes wrong, prepare your response. Will you be disappointed, or will you go with the flow? Will you be angry or instead choose empathy? The more you can anticipate pitfalls, the better prepared you will be!

Notes and Thoughts

CHAPTER 18

MRS. BIG

Her name was Linda, and she scared the hell out of me.

It began twenty years ago. Linda showed up a few minutes late for a board meeting, walked in confidently, dropped her briefcase on the empty chair next to her, and immediately joined the conversation that had already begun.

Linda was successful, outspoken, and intimidating.

And I really wanted her to be my client.

She owned a big company in an industry otherwise dominated by men. Her employees loved and respected her, as did our community. She was one of those people who would tell you the truth even if you didn't ask for feedback.

Linda was practical—which is also how she ran her business. I liked her and felt we shared many similarities. We were both smart, we cared about many of the same things, and I wholeheartedly believed I was the right person to give her guidance about her money, her planning, and her philanthropy.

There was only one problem. I was too afraid to call her.

Then two years went by.

Over coffee one morning with my client Anne, we were brainstorming possible sponsors for an upcoming fundraiser, and Anne mentioned Linda.

"You should ask Linda about sponsoring the event. She's your client, right?" Anne assumed.

"No. But I wish she were," I said, a little embarrassed.

"Why isn't she? Aren't you on the board of the foundation together? Don't you have a bunch of friends in common? She seems like she'd be the perfect client for you." Anne was perplexed.

"Linda scares me," I confessed.

"She scares you? That is hilarious! I mean, you don't exactly come across as the kind of person who's easily intimidated. And isn't that the secret sauce in your business? Don't you have to be willing to pick up the phone and call people if you want to make a living?"

"That's true."

"Then call her! In fact, I want you to promise me you will call her by the end of the day on Friday."

Throughout my career, I rarely experienced "call reluctance." Anne was right: If you want to survive in the financial planning business, you must be willing to pick up the phone and call people regardless of how you feel. As

I have learned over and over, **sometimes our feelings are irrelevant**. We must do what's necessary to make it in this business, regardless of how uncomfortable it makes us feel.

For whatever reason, Linda seemed unapproachable to me. She was what we used to refer to as a "Mr. Big"— except I suppose Mrs. Big would be more appropriate. For years, no matter how much I grew in my business and gained confidence, skills, and knowledge, I still had not picked up the phone to call Linda.

But I accepted Anne's challenge.

I waited until the end of the day on Friday to make the call. I dialed Linda's number and immediately prayed for voicemail.

Linda picked up the phone. I awkwardly announced my name and then started to explain who I was. She cut me off.

"Amy, I know who you are." She laughed in a surprisingly friendly way. "What can I do for you?"

I asked her to have lunch. She instantly agreed. No objections. We picked a date for the following week. **It was simple**.

A week later, we met. I got to the restaurant early and waited at a table by the window. I saw Linda walking toward the front entrance. I was nervous, and my hands were clammy. I wiped them on my pants, hoping to dry them quickly enough so I could shake her hand.

Linda spotted me, walked over to the table, and— wait for it—**she hugged me**! As if we were old friends.

Before she could say a word, I blurted out, "Thanks so much for agreeing to meet with me. I need to share something…I have been avoiding calling you for years." As I listened to the words I was saying, they all felt awkward.

"Me? Why?" she asked.

This was my moment of truth and vulnerability.

"I have always been intimidated by you." Her eyes widened. That's when I realized, perhaps I should have kept that statement to myself.

"Intimidated?" She looked horrified. "Oh, my goodness, I'm so sorry! Please tell me what I did to intimidate you. I feel terrible."

She waited for my response.

I back-pedaled. "Oh no, sorry, you didn't do a thing! It's me. I have such respect for you as a business owner. I have always wanted to work with you. I just never had the courage to call you and tell you that."

"So what changed? I mean, after all this time, why did you suddenly call me last week?"

"Well, you know our mutual friend Anne…the truth is, I promised Anne that I would call you. Your name came up in conversation last week, and she assumed you were my client. When I told her you were not—and that I had **been afraid to call you** for years—she could not believe it. In fact, she made me promise that I would call you before the end of the day last Friday." I paused awkwardly and took a breath. "So here we are."

She laughed. Like, belly laughed—and loudly—as if the whole thing were so absurd to her.

That was it. **Ice broken**.

Fast-forward to last weekend. Linda, her spouse, and I were reminiscing about how long we had known each other. That's when I realized that they have both been my clients for more than twenty years. We have shared dinners and events and milestones, extreme highs and lows, and even went on a vacation together. Linda knew me before my son was born, and I knew both of her parents before they passed.

When Linda sold her company, I had the privilege of being one of her advisors and confidantes throughout the process. Yes, we are colleagues . . . but we are also friends. To this day, she is one of my favorite people on the planet.

Ironically, Mrs. Big turned out to be a regular person: someone with goals, a need for a plan, and a vision for her future. Yes, she was smart and successful—but she was also someone without a financial advisor until I finally called her.

We have been on an incredible journey together. She grew her business at the same time I grew mine. Our respect and admiration for each other are mutual. I'm grateful for our relationship—and appreciative that Anne saw through my excuses and challenged me to make that call.

It made a gigantic difference for both me and Linda.

Think about the person you've been reluctant to reach out to. Maybe it's a potential business partner you could collaborate with but aren't sure how to start the conversation. **So you haven't yet.** Maybe there's someone you want to set up on a blind date with your best friend, but you haven't figured out how to approach either of them. Who is your Mr. Big or Mrs. Big?

Promise me you will call them by the end of the day on Friday.

Ideas to Spark, Connect & Create this week:

- Think back over time to your personal and professional relationships. Are there people you admire and would like to get to know better? List their names.
- Pick one of the people above and commit to connecting with them in the next week.
- Think about your business or community involvement. There must be people on your wish list you would love to have as clients, connections, or even potential donors for your organization. Who comes to mind first and foremost? List their names.
- Pick one of the people above and commit to connecting with them in the next week.

Notes and Thoughts

CHAPTER 19

FIRST IN, LAST OUT

My dad used to tell me that his best work got done early in the morning before anyone else showed up at the office. He also believed in these principles:

- Be proud of the work you do.
- Try to learn something new every day.
- Take great care of your people, and they will take care of you.

I took that advice to heart when I became a financial advisor in 1997. It started with my being the first person to the office every morning. I'd pull into a completely empty parking garage. I would park in my usual spot. At that time of morning, there were no other cars there besides the one belonging to the security guard.

I vividly remember the walk from the empty garage to the door of the building, carrying my stiff new leather briefcase. I would disarm the alarm, turn on all the lights, and make my way to my cubicle. I also carried a travel mug filled with my morning coffee. As a brand-new financial advisor, I had no extra dollars for the Dunkin' Donuts drive-thru. My thinking was that every extra hour I spent working on my business and every dollar I *didn't* spend buying to-go coffee would all eventually make a difference someday.

My cubicle had one of those green bank lights with a gold chain. Every cubicle looked the same. I would spend the first two hours of my day prepping my client files. Then I would drive to my clients' houses, where I would meet with them at their kitchen tables and ask about their dreams and goals and priorities. At the end of the day, I would return to the office to complete my forms, print out hundreds of pieces of paper, and then use the binding machine to carefully put the clients' plans together in a neat package.

I had no help in the beginning. I served as the advisor as well as my own assistant. When the "workday" was done, I would spend another hour or two finishing calls, tidying up paperwork, and prepping for the next day—all under the green glow of my desk lamp. Even back in those early days of uncertainty and insecurity, I loved the work. I loved helping clients. And I committed to doing whatever it took to build a successful business over the long-term.

I reminded myself all the time of my vision: to one day be able to buy my own building with an actual office (upgrade from a cubicle), to be able to hire an awesome team of people, and to no longer need to be the first into the office.

In the beginning, not only was I first in, but I was usually the last one out as well.

At the end of each day, I'd turn off my desk lamp, pack up my briefcase, shut off the lights and set the building alarm. I remember feeling a sense of pride after a productive day, following my dad's advice, and hoping that one day I would "make it."

My dad was young when he started his own business. He and his partner were in their early twenties. They committed to working hard to build the business together, treating their employees like family, and taking excellent care of their customers. Eventually, Dad and Ed were able to buy their own building, expand, and experience the pride of successful self-employment.

As a child, I can still remember my dad leaving the house early for his job. And on the weekends in the summer, he would return to his shop to mow the lawn, pull the weeds, and make sure the place looked tidy before everyone else returned on Monday morning. All those details mattered to him. To him, the office work and the lawn care were all parts of his job. He was so proud of his work, his business, his property, and his employees. He talked about it all the time.

I've been thinking about the simple but poignant lessons from my dad that have stuck with me all these years. My dad passed away on May 4, 1998, a month shy of his fifty-first birthday. If you asked anyone who knew him, they'd tell you he was the guy who had it all—and the guy who was least likely to die prematurely. His death didn't make any sense to me back then. I was only twenty-six years old, in my second year as a financial advisor. I had been trained to be prepared for the death of a client and how to handle the death claim process and the family. I just never expected the client would be my dad, and the family I'd have to help was my own.

And now, almost twenty-five years later, I was first to my office this morning, channeling those lessons from my dad from so long ago. Before heading into my building, I walked across my parking lot, pulled a couple of weeds out from the fresh mulch that the landscapers delivered last week, and poured some water into the flowerpot on my front porch. Then I unlocked the door, shut off the alarm, and turned all the lights on. My routine has not changed that much after all these years . . .

But my life has.

Instead of work being stressful and uncertain, I now show up confident and clear. My dream of one day owning my own building came true. I still work with clients I love, and I still look forward to sitting down with them to ask about their goals and priorities. Instead of having to do the work myself, I have an amazing team of dedicated people who care as much about the clients as I do.

At the end of the day—even now—I am often the last one out. Those final few minutes before leaving the office give me a chance to walk through the building, shut off the lights in each room, and appreciate what we have built together as a team. I pause for a quick moment of gratitude before locking up the door, setting the alarm, and heading home.

I often wonder what my life would be like if my dad were still alive. It is impossible to know. But what I can be certain of is this: My team and I will continue to show up early, work together to help as many awesome clients as we can, and be proud of the work we do. We will appreciate the new things we continue to learn and vow to always treat our clients and each other like family.

It does not matter if you are the business owner or if you are the newest employee at someone else's company. Occasionally, show up first to work. Appreciate the quiet time you have to yourself in the early morning before the hustle and bustle begins.

I recommend that you occasionally stay after hours once everyone else leaves. Give yourself that moment to be proud of who you are, what you do, and those you have helped today.

I am sure my dad would appreciate your efforts.

Ideas to Spark, Connect & Create this week:

- Are you someone still new to your career? Still needing to get in early, work late, and continue to prove yourself? Take time to write down the vision you have for yourself in five years. List your accomplishments, skills, credentials, and maybe even lighter work schedule due to your success. Read this vision often.
- Are you someone successful in your career? It could be a corporate job, a service job, or your success as a parent. Take a few minutes to write down the work you are proud of. Reflect on the hard work that got you here, the skills you've developed over time, and the impact you have had on so many people—yourself included.
- Are you the boss or the person in charge of your department? Do you see young people new in their jobs and struggling to make it, fit in, and be successful? Take time to notice them. Comment on the fact that you see how early they show up and how late they leave. Encourage their work ethic—and let them know that hard work **always eventually** pays off.

Notes and Thoughts

CHAPTER 20

THE TIES THAT BIND

In 2020, Bruce Springsteen was asked to be the musical guest on *Saturday Night Live*. Even though it was a year with no live music or tours due to the pandemic, Bruce Springsteen and the E Street Band got on the *SNL* stage and crushed it!

To watch them perform is to witness passion in action. Each member of the band puts their heart and soul into every song. They sing the lyrics like that's their favorite song, despite how many thousands of times they've performed it before.

Watching them on television brought me back to my first Springsteen concert. I had never been a huge fan, but I had heard about how epic his concerts are. Kim and I went with our friends Jeff, Howie, and Scott. Jeff had seen The Boss eleven times. Howie had been to nineteen shows. And Scott was there for his twenty-sixth. These were *fans*. They were so excited for Kim and me to have this first-timer experience.

We watched and listened as the band played all twenty tracks, in order, from their famous double album *The River*. The fans—true Springsteen fans—sang **every word to every song**. They belted the lyrics out the way Bruce did, with passion and enthusiasm. And this continued nonstop for three and a half hours.

I loved every moment of it.

As I watched them perform again, this time on *Saturday Night Live*, I was brought back to the feeling I had at the concert. I have to admit, I even got a little choked up. To watch Bruce command the stage and deliver a stellar performance while in his seventies is amazing. Next to him was his wife of thirty-plus years, Patti Scialfa—still rocking her long red hair and tight leather pants—as well as his loyal friend Steven Van Zandt (also known for his role of Silvio on *The Sopranos*), who's also in his seventies but still looks and sounds awesome.

And then there's the "young" guy playing the sax, Jake Clemons, in his thirties and the nephew of the late Clarence Clemons. Clarence died in 2011 and left his beloved saxophone *Excalibur* to Jake. Jake replaced his uncle in the E Street Band but claims, "Even though I'm playing his saxophone now, make no mistake, Clarence is still on that stage with us every night."

Bruce Springsteen and the E Street Band's history and continued success are admirable. Think about it: To have had the same job for forty-plus years, to love the work so much, to perform alongside talented people decade after decade, to be friends with (or even married to) your bandmates, and to continue to get better with time—who doesn't aspire to all of that?

I've always seen Bruce Springsteen as a superstar. A legend. A musical success. But it was not until his performance on *SNL* that I began to see him as a **role model**. I didn't realize it until now, but **I aspire to be like The Boss**.

I'm no rock star—and you certainly don't want to hear me sing—but all the elements that are present on his stage are the things I strive for every day. Creating a legacy. Showing up for every client meeting I have with passion. Demonstrating a love for my craft. Acquiring and keeping loyal "fans" for decades. Having endurance and getting better with age. Being enthusiastic and passionate every time I show up. And having the privilege of working alongside people I love, which is so much more fun than being a solo artist. **Yeah, I want to be like The Boss**.

For me, this was a revelation. But for those of you who are lifelong Springsteen fans, you probably already know this. After all, these are the ties that bind.

Ideas to Spark, Connect & Create this week:

- Take a moment to assess your craft, whether it's your job, your role as a parent or a spouse, your position on a nonprofit board of directors, etc. Choose one example from the many roles you play and take time to assess how refined your skills are in this area. Do you bring enthusiasm, passion, and love to this role? Are you tired of the mundane tasks associated with it? Have you been doing it so long, it's now happening on autopilot?
- Once you have picked a role you play, list below some elements of the "job" that you happen to be great at. What are you proud of? What lights you up?
- Are there other areas where you have become stale, and you could brush up your skills, learn something new, or put some much-needed pep in your step?
- Over the next week, what will you put extra effort into? Which role or job is worth investing in first?

Notes and Thoughts

CHAPTER 21

SEEK TO UNDERSTAND

My niece BB and I were painting rocks together. She particularly liked my rainbow rock and told me I should put it on my front steps for Pride Month. Surprised by her comment, I asked her what she knew about Pride Month.

BB shared with me that she had recently joined the Pride Committee at her school. They were spending time preparing activities for students in the hopes that more kids would learn what Pride Month is all about. When I asked her what Pride Month means to her—a nine-year-old—BB said quite confidently, "Pride means people can love who they love, just like you and Auntie Kimmy. It means people can choose to use whatever pronouns they feel comfortable with. And you can be straight or gay or transgender. It doesn't matter. We just need to accept people the way they are."

At age nine, BB's interpretation of Pride Month is about kindness. And all I could think was how incredible her school is for making such a special effort to teach lessons of understanding and acceptance to their community.

I, too, have been thinking about Pride Month and what it means.

I brought it up with my colleague Bailey. She told me about something that had just happened with her eight-year-old daughter, Mila. Mila is in second grade, and last week her class had a substitute teacher—a transgender woman. This was a new experience for her daughter, who understandably came home with some questions. Mila asked her mom if it was "okay" for a teacher to look kind of like a man but also wear makeup. Bailey answered her daughter's questions thoughtfully and factually, and Mila seemed satisfied with her answers. Bailey assumed that was the end of the conversation. But it wasn't.

On Friday, Bailey received an email from the substitute teacher. Apparently, Mila approached the teacher to let her know that she thought her makeup looked beautiful. The teacher emailed Bailey to let her know what a kind and accepting daughter she has—and that it meant the world to receive such a compliment, especially from a child. The teacher shared that she is in the beginning stages of her transition from male to female and commented that many people are unsure how to react to her. Mila's kindness and empathy, however, were so encouraging.

This got me thinking: If eight- and nine-year-old kids can ask authentic questions, be curious, seek to understand, and ultimately choose to show kindness—doesn't it seem like adults could do this more often too?

You may be asking, "Does this really matter? Is this *necessary*?"

Does it matter on a Zoom call when the moderator updates his name to include "him/his" pronouns, even though most people on the call know he identifies as male? It might not matter to you, but for the one gender-nonconforming colleague on that Zoom call to suddenly feel comfortable adding "they/them" next to their own name for the first time ever—yes, you bet it matters.

I recently overheard a man at a conference ask his colleagues if they thought Pride Month should be a thing. "I mean, is it necessary to carve a whole month out for gay people to wave their flags and show their pride?" A black man in the group responded instantly: "Well, bro, you might ask the same thing about Juneteenth, and I'll tell you that acknowledging June 19 matters for my family and me. I imagine Pride Month gives the same kind of acknowledgment to gay people."

If these stories spark interest and you find yourself nodding in agreement, keep reading.

And if these examples are uncomfortable for you, I encourage you to keep reading as well.

You may not feel any connection to this subject. I get it. You may have zero reasons for celebrating Pride Month. Totally understandable. But be aware that there is a pretty good chance this topic will hit home for you someday. It is possible that your child or a close friend or your coworker might someday come out to you. How you react in that moment could make a profound difference for them—positive or negative. You get to choose. And you can also be prepared.

I'm writing today about Pride Month to help bring awareness to the topic—and to help you be more prepared for the moment when someone starts this conversation with you. Your kindness and acceptance will matter. I promise you.

This is exactly what happened to my friend last year. He called me and sounded upset.

"Are you okay?" I asked.

"I need your help. My daughter just told us she is gay. I'm not sure I handled it very well." My friend paused. He stumbled over his words a bit. "I mean, I definitely told her that we love her and that we are always going to be here to support her . . . but I still feel like I should have said something else. Something better. Honestly, I wasn't prepared for this."

This past year has been quite a journey—not only for his daughter but for their whole family. They've all figured out how to get more comfortable, ask more questions, and learn to be more open-minded than they already were—all in an effort to better understand and support their loved one. They were seeking to understand. Believe me when I tell you that this family exudes support, love, and pride. And not surprising, their daughter is thriving as a result.

How we treat people is a choice. I am not writing today to judge you for your beliefs. I am simply asking you to pause, think, and choose your words and reactions carefully when it comes to others. I am also asking that you try a little harder. Referring to someone with their new pronouns takes some extra effort. Let us all make that effort.

At some point, someone you care about may choose to share their vulnerable, life-changing news with you. Your reaction to their announcement can make a profound difference in their self-esteem and their confidence. What if you used this reminder and took this very moment—well in advance—to prepare for how you will react to that person in the future?

Every June, we recognize Pride Month. Members of the LGBTQ+ community will be taking the time to celebrate their relationships, rejoice in their ability to get married legally in our country and reflect on how far they've come.

From the bottom of my heart, thank you in advance for respecting this month of joy. Thank you for teaching the children in your life what Pride means.

Parents, thank you for the effort you are making to raise kind and accepting kids. And let us all give a special shout-out to parents of LGBTQ+ kids—you are remarkable humans, raising remarkable humans.

Thank you, readers, for seeking to understand.

And to Jane, this chapter is dedicated to you and your brave journey.

Ideas to Spark, Connect & Create this week:

- Do you know someone in the LGBTQ+ community? Have you ever taken the time to ask about their coming out story? What if this week you reached out and did that? It doesn't necessarily have to be Pride Month. Now is a fine time.
- Is there someone you know—either close to you or not—who is going through a gender transition, questioning their sexuality, or has recently changed their pronouns? What if you reach out to see how they are doing and offer to be someone open and accepting, someone who is willing to listen? The difference your kindness makes could be monumental to that person.

Notes and Thoughts

CHAPTER 22

LOOKING FOR A NEW KIM?

I read an article about a homing pigeon named "New Kim." Apparently, in Belgium, there is a competitive market for purchasing prize pigeons at auction. As explained in an article in *The New York Times*, "In this sport, which dates back to at least the 1800s, homing pigeons are acclimated in a shared loft before being taken hundreds of miles away and released; the winner is the first to return."[5] New Kim is a two-year-old female pigeon—and apparently quite good at her job. How do we know this? Because two Chinese business people engaged in a bidding war over her at an auction, and the winner paid $1.9 million.

For a pigeon.

As a financial advisor, I found myself starting to calculate how much impact $1.9 million could have had on this buyer's retirement plan. Then two things occurred to me:

1. If you can afford $1.9 million for a pigeon, you're probably not too worried about your retirement.
2. In the words of my coach Dan Sullivan, "Sometimes we want what we want."

Have you ever wanted something just because you wanted it? With no reason or logical justification?

When I was in my twenties, I wanted a Rolex watch. Growing up, I had always believed that a Rolex watch was a symbol of success. At that time, I was a recently divorced young mother. My business was in its early years and not profitable (at all). I was living in a one-bedroom apartment with a cat and leasing a Toyota Camry. I hadn't even considered contributing to a 401(k) yet. Of course, the last thing I needed was an overpriced, materialistic wristwatch.

But I wanted it.

And I wanted it so much that I made it my mission to work extra hours and save money systematically for six months with a laser focus on obtaining my prized possession.

I went to the jewelry store, picked out the exact Rolex I wanted, and told the woman behind the counter that I'd be back in six months. Every Friday, I would leave my office at the end of the workday, walk across Main

Street, and try the watch on. I had to have it, and as time went on, I felt like I was truly earning it. I sacrificed other things along the way to make certain I could afford to buy it. And I calculated every dollar I made and put aside each week what was needed to ultimately afford the watch.

Six months later, it was mine. I had enough money in my checking account to write a check for it (no debit cards back then). I signed my name on the check and could not be prouder!

To this day, I love the watch and what it still symbolizes for me. But at the time, no one would have understood why I wanted it.

Sometimes we want what we want. And we don't have to explain or justify it to anyone else.

I have a friend who recently bought a $250,000 sports car. It is gorgeous. No one in our city has one like it. Recently I saw it was parked out in front of a local restaurant. I heard passersby comment quietly, "Do you know how many other useful, practical things that guy could have done with the money he spent on that car?" Not that the stranger even knew whose car it was. Their comments were as generic and judgmental as my New Kim pigeon comments.

The good news is that public opinion is completely irrelevant to my fast-car-driving friend. The joy and happiness he experiences when driving his car every day is worth every penny to him—even if no one else understands. **And he doesn't feel the need to explain this to anyone**.

Some people spend money on collectibles, artwork, purebred labradoodles, a big house, numerous advanced degrees, lavish vacations, fine wine—you name it, there is something someone else has, **and you do not understand for a second why they have chosen to spend money on it**.

You wonder, "Why would anyone spend money on that _____?"

You know what? It doesn't matter.

Because sometimes we simply want what we want.

What gets tricky is when people want something but don't move forward with the purchase or the acquisition or the adventure—simply because they are worried about what others think. Instead, they deprive themselves of it as a result.

Does this sound like you?

Disclaimer: I'm a financial advisor. I am not suggesting you cash in your 401(k) for a Ferrari. However, I *am* a big proponent of having a dream, making a plan, and achieving whatever it is you want...even if no one else understands it but you.

Ideas to Spark, Connect & Create this week:

- What's the thing you really want to do, see, purchase or experience—even though you don't *need* it?
- What's holding you back? Are you worried about what others will say?
- Why does that matter? Write down the answer to this question. I bet it will surprise you.
- Did you consider that others might admire you for having the guts to go for it?
- Over the next week, your challenge is to make some progress toward achieving or acquiring that thing you wish you had. Try on the watch. Test drive the car. Search Zillow for the dream house. What will you dare to take on in the next seven days?

Notes and Thoughts

CHAPTER 23

STAY IN YOUR LANE

I went out with my mom last week. She offered to be the driver. She picked me up at my house, and we headed out on a shopping adventure.

We were in the middle of a conversation when her car made a loud *beep, beep, beep* sound. I checked to be sure our seatbelts were on. They were.

Again, beep, beep, beep.

"What's that noise?" I asked. Mom explained that her new Subaru was equipped with a beeping alarm to notify the driver anytime they crossed over a line in the road.

As Mom took the next curve, her tires veered slightly over the middle line, only for a second, and again there was the *beep, beep, beep* noise to remind her: *Stay in your lane.*

We drove forty-five minutes to the shopping plaza. Throughout our journey, her car periodically had to remind her to get back into the center of her lane. I found it to be a helpful, albeit annoying, safety feature.

Later in the week, I was at the office working. I logged into a spreadsheet that tracks all the work our team is engaged in. It's very detail oriented. Everyone on the team contributes to it, so we all are aware of what's happening with each of our projects. It's not a spreadsheet I typically utilize. My role is to stay focused on the big picture, and the Excel sheet is for the team to manage the details of their workflows.

As I scrolled through the very complex sheet, I started rethinking ways to format the data, change the font, switch up the colors, and simplify it. As I was changing the shade of green in the heading, I swear I could hear that beeping noise from my mom's car: **Stay in your lane**.

I realized in that moment that I was venturing into territory that was not mine. The spreadsheet was not part of my job responsibility. In fact, it was not even created by me! I had no business interfering in it, changing it, or switching it up.

I immediately exited the document without saving my random changes. Instead, I returned to the work I was supposed to be doing.

Later that afternoon, I needed a little break from my computer screen and took a walk around the office. I thought, *I might as well water the plants*. This is not something I normally do, but I thought I'd be helpful. I located the watering can and started with the large plant in our lobby. I completely oversaturated it. I also flooded the dish it was sitting in and needed many paper towels to clean up my mess. Apparently, all the plants had already been watered that morning—like always. While sopping up the water now flowing across the floor, I was instantly reminded that I was not the person in charge of the plants. *Beep, beep, beep.* There I was, drifting out of my lane again.

Safety features on cars are designed specifically to keep the driver safe. Too bad we as humans don't come equipped with those warnings too.

Wouldn't it be great if we came programmed with a little sensor that reminded us periodically to stay in our lane? How often do we take on things that are not our business? Do you find yourself straying into other people's areas with good intentions—probably even genuinely meaning to help them—but then realize that staying in your own lane is the better, safer place? For everyone?

Sometimes we drift out of our lane in an effort to contribute or be useful, like my friend who decided to mow the lawn when her husband was working late, only to get his tractor completely stuck in the mud on the hill behind their house. Instead of *being helpful*, she ended up *needing help* to get towed out of the mud she buried the tractor wheels in. Mowing the lawn just wasn't her lane.

Beep, beep, beep. Get back in your lane! Next time you're thinking of taking something on that's not really your job, your responsibility, or even your business, think of Mom's car. And trust that staying in your lane is likely a safer, less disruptive place for you to remain.

Ideas to Spark, Connect & Create this week:

- Look around at different areas in your life. Where are you drifting out of your lane?
- In an effort to be "helpful," have you drifted into someone else's lane? Do you owe them an apology and a promise to stay out of their way in the future?
- What is *your* lane? Take some time to define this for yourself since it can change over the years. Once you identify the area(s) you excel and thrive, you'll be happy to spend more time in those other lanes.

Notes and Thoughts

CHAPTER 24

CONFETTI MOMENTS

It was my son Charlie's twenty-first birthday. I wanted to do something special with him, just the two of us. I asked him to be prepared for a long car ride that would end with lunch at any restaurant he chose.

We started our adventure at 9:00 a.m. on Monday morning. When he got in the car, I handed him a piece of paper that had twenty-one locations listed on it. He questioned what we were doing and why Baystate Hospital was at the top of the list.

I explained to Charlie that I was taking him on a "This Is Your Life So Far" tour and that it was obviously starting at the hospital where he was born.

He was skeptical.

As we drove the fifteen minutes to the hospital parking lot, I shared with him how much I loved being pregnant with him, and I didn't know until he was born that I was going to have a baby boy. I told him what it was like to be a new mother to a preemie baby, that he was only five pounds at birth, and that he spent the first four weeks of his life in the NICU. I shared about my worries initially and then how excited I was when he was finally healthy enough to come home.

Charlie was quiet but listening.

From there, we drove to the house we first lived in. I pointed out the dogwood tree in the front yard that was planted in memory of my father. I explained to Charlie the house would always hold a special place in my heart because it's where we spent our first year together and where I painted the mural on the wall in his nursery.

Charlie began opening up and sharing stories and feelings about his childhood. We had a twenty-minute ride to our next stop: his nursery school. We talked non stop the whole way there. He shared memories I didn't even know he had, and I shared stories I had never told him before.

We proceeded to drive past his kindergarten, middle school, junior high, and high school. In between, we drove past all the basketball courts he played on, the house where he learned to ride a two-wheeler, his summer camp, and each of his favorite local restaurants. He reminisced about a few other places that weren't on my list, and we drove past those, too. All the while, we shared memories and funny stories about the past twenty-one years.

At the end of our three-hour tour, Charlie turned to me and said, "That was actually pretty cool. I wasn't really sure at the beginning what the point of all this was going to be."

I parked the car in the parking lot of the restaurant he chose.

Then he hugged me.

"Thanks for all this, Mom. For real. This was a cool way to start my day. I hadn't thought about those places in a long time. It reminded me of what a fun childhood I had. I have to be honest. You were a really strict mom growing up, and I'm not gonna lie—that sometimes sucked for me. But you always kept pushing me to do better. Now I understand why you were that way with me: You just wanted me to try harder and do better and be successful. **I get it now**."

I sat next to my son in the car, listening to the words he was saying, feeling so incredibly grateful and thinking, *This is a confetti moment.*

A confetti moment is a very personal time in life when you feel profound joy, happiness, surprise, and celebration. It's often not something an outsider cares about as much as you do. And it's not grand like a graduation or a wedding. What I'm referring to are the smaller, more subtle times in life where you think, *Cue the confetti because something terrific is happening to me right now.*

That moment, alone with my son in the car, was a real confetti moment for me. **And apparently, it was for him too**.

I shared this concept with a group of friends over dinner, and I asked them what confetti moments came to mind. These were some of their immediate replies:

- **When my daughter lost her first tooth**: The excitement on her face, the anticipation of the tooth fairy coming, all of it. If I had confetti, it would have been the moment to toss it over both of us to make the moment complete.
- **Getting my driver's license**: I will never forget the moment I got in the car alone, pulled out of the driveway, and felt a freedom like I had never felt before. (You can feel it, too, right? Cue the confetti.)
- **Performing in the high school play**: I was so nervous on the opening night of the play. But I remembered all my lines. I felt like I belonged up there. The months of rehearsals suddenly felt worth it. And when I finished my solo, I got a standing ovation. That was a confetti moment for me, for sure.
- **The day my son left for the US Marines**: I had been a nervous wreck planning for that day, helping him pack, and trying not to show my emotions. When he came down the stairs in his uniform, ready to leave, I had never felt so proud in my life. I can still feel it to this day. It was one of my hardest but best mom moments. (Can you feel that too? Cue the confetti.)

Other notable confetti moments included the one when Sasha's puppy finally learned to sit on command at puppy school graduation, and the day Mike and Michelle got the call that there was a baby ready for adoption, and when Jackson got to ring the bell at the hospital signifying that his cancer was officially in remission. Personal, proud, profound little moments, each of them!

We have all experienced these special times. But as soon as I gave the feeling a name—**a confetti moment**—I started to become much more aware of them. I began recognizing confetti possibilities in the smallest things, like the tiny cucumber growing on the vine that wasn't there the day before, but appeared magically overnight. All I could think was, "I grew that! It took all summer, but there's the reward. Cue the confetti!"

Confetti moments are personal experiences that bring up feelings of excitement, pride, happiness, joy, or connection. They're special, and even better when the moment is shared with someone else.

So thank you, Charlie, for that special day and for allowing me to share your story. Love, Mom.

Ideas to Spark, Connect & Create this week:

- When was the last time you experienced a confetti moment?
- When was the last time you made a confetti moment happen for someone else?

- Take time this week to be more mindful of the small joys and celebrations happening right in front of you.
- Better yet, take time this week to make a confetti moment happen for someone you love: Bring your nephew for a double scoop ice cream cone, take your grandmother for a ride in your convertible, or send a thank-you note to someone who would never expect it.

Notes and Thoughts

CHAPTER 25

TEAMWORK IS CRITICAL

I got a notification that the burglar alarm sounded in our office building at 2:16 a.m. Monday. The good news: no actual burglar. The bad news: The security camera showed some type of bird flapping around **inside** our building, which had apparently triggered the alarm.

I arrived at work extra early on Monday to deal with the situation. I was relieved when my sister Nicki (our bookkeeper) arrived at the same time. I warned her that we might encounter a bird as we were walking into the office. Together we scouted out each room on the first floor, and all seemed well. No sign of a bird, nor any bird-related damage.

We headed upstairs to where my office is. It was instantly apparent that the air conditioner had stopped working on the second floor. The thermostat said it was eighty-nine degrees. I started sweating, still moving cautiously, and searching for the bird. There was no sign of any foul play within my office. The hallway was clear. Same for the kitchen.

But when we turned the corner to Nicki's office, there it was, nestled in between the window fan and the screen. And it was not a bird . . .

It was a bat.

And it was sleeping. I may have screamed a little.

I quickly closed the door to Nicki's office so we could discuss what to do next. That's when I also heard other people from our team arriving at the office for what they thought was a normal Monday. Five of us gathered in the kitchen outside Nicki's office, thinking about a strategy.

We called pest control, only to be informed they don't "do bats."

Mice, *yes*.

Bugs, *yes*.

Bats, *no*.

We had to take the matter into our own hands. Nicki put on the kitchen rubber gloves we use to wash dishes, and I grabbed the biggest serrated knife we had. Together we opened the door to her office. There was the bat, still hanging quietly in the window.

It's worth noting here: **I am petrified of bats**.

Despite that, I knew we weren't going to do anything that would hurt him. The goal was to figure out how to open the screen to let him out safely. But we couldn't do it from the outside because we had no ladder to get to the second floor. If we tried to pop the screen out from the inside, we risked the bat flying in, not out.

Too chancy.

We decided we'd attempt to release the bat through the screen by cutting it (the screen, not the bat). I very slowly approached the window. I held the knife in one hand. I held my sister's hand with the other. She was still wearing rubber gloves.

Luckily, the knife was really sharp, and I was able to carefully slice through the screen on the right side of the bat effortlessly. He didn't budge. He was still wedged between the screen and the window fan.

Next, I sliced through the screen on the left side of him, no problem. Now we had two parallel cuts in the screen on either side of him. The last step was to make a final cut across the top of the screen to create a flap, and hopefully, that would be enough to release him safely to the outside.

Don't forget, it was eighty-nine degrees *inside* the office. I was sweating. Nicki was sweating. Jessica was taking pictures of the entire scene (definitely not included in this book, mostly to save all of us from embarrassment).

Nicki shuffled closer to the window and was able to slide it up a little higher with the grip of her rubber gloves. This slight move loosened the fan just enough to give me space to make the final cut across the top of the screen with my knife.

In one swoop, I sliced open the screen, the flap fell forward, the bat woke up, and he flew outside. Nicki grabbed the fan before it fell out the window. The screen was destroyed, but we all agreed it seemed like a very small price to pay for the bat mission we had successfully completed.

I would never have anticipated that Monday morning would include a burglar alarm, a knife, a bat, and some screaming.

I'm chalking the whole encounter up to teamwork. We rallied, shared some genius ideas, worked as a group, and figured out how to fix the dilemma pretty darn quickly.

Since then, the air conditioner has been repaired, the screen has been replaced, and our team is back in business.

Ideas to Spark, Connect & Create this week:

- When was the last time you were asked to do something at work, and, although you fulfilled the request, you felt some resentment? Like, *that's not in my job description*. What if, instead, the next time you're asked to pitch in for something out of the scope of your normal job, you enthusiastically respond? Just try this. You might be surprised at how much easier the task at hand becomes.

- When was the last time you asked someone to do something at work that wasn't in their job description? Did you give them an enthusiastic thank you afterward? If not, it's not too late to go back and mention how much you appreciated their teamwork and willingness to help.
- The next time you're at work or at a friend's house and you see something you could do to help out or pitch in, do it without hesitation. Sometimes unsolicited support is just what the other person needs.

Notes and Thoughts

CHAPTER 26

COMMIT AND MOVE FORWARD

What does it truly mean to commit?

I thought about this after a friend posted an article about the guards of the Tomb of the Unknown Soldier.[6] It has been decades since I have had a civics class, so it wasn't surprising that I did not remember many of these fascinating details:

- Guards are changed every thirty minutes, twenty-four hours a day, 365 days a year.
- For people to apply for guard duty at the tomb, they must commit two years of their life to guard the tomb, live in a barracks under the tomb, and are not allowed to drink alcohol, on or off duty, *for the rest of their lives.*
- They cannot swear in public for the rest of their lives.
- They cannot disgrace the uniform or the tomb in any way.

- After two years, the guard is given a wreath pin that is worn on their lapel, signifying they served as a guard of the tomb. There are only 400 presently worn. The guard must obey these rules for the rest of their lives or give up the wreath pin.
- During the first six months of duty, a guard cannot talk to anyone nor watch TV. Instead, all off-duty time is spent studying the 175 notable people laid to rest in Arlington National Cemetery. A guard must memorize this information.
- Every guard spends **five hours a day** getting his uniforms ready for guard duty.
- The tomb has been patrolled continuously, 24/7, since 1930.
- In 2003 as Hurricane Isabelle was approaching Washington, DC, our US Senate and House took two days off in anticipation of the storm. On the ABC evening news, it was reported that because of the dangers of the hurricane, the military members assigned the duty of guarding the Tomb of the Unknown Soldier were given permission to suspend the assignment. They respectfully declined the offer. They said that guarding the tomb was not just an assignment—it was the highest honor that can be afforded to a service person.

Serving in this capacity is an incredible example of someone making a conscious decision to commit despite how unpleasant or challenging the details might be.

Think about the level of commitment an elite athlete makes. My brother-in-law David Henry is a professional bodybuilder and has been for the past twenty years. His focus and dedication to his sport are impressive. What he is willing to sacrifice during his training season every year is commendable. Each exercise in every workout is tracked, and every ounce of food he consumes is calculated and measured. Dave has full commitment to his sport.

Throughout our lives, we are all faced with commitment choices, big and small. Your religion may ask you to commit to their Ten Commandments, to not work on the Sabbath, or to prepare all your food in a very particular and symbolic way. Maybe you are asked to faithfully wed the person your parents arranged for you to marry. These are all big commitments.

Smaller commitments include meeting deadlines as promised, being someone your boss can rely on, and showing up at the gym on time to meet your workout buddy.

Big or small, keeping commitments demonstrates character. Take a look at the commitments you have kept. What was it about them that had you stick to them? Now take a moment to reflect on commitments in the past that you have *not managed to keep*. What was different about those?

As you move forward, be mindful of the significant number of commitments being asked of you and remember to choose wisely. Wouldn't you rather be known as a person who commits and sticks with their promise rather than someone who overcommits and is unreliable?

The guard for the Tomb of the Unknown Soldier is a great role model: Know what you are getting into before you commit, then once you choose to move forward, do a stellar job.

Ideas to Spark, Connect & Create this week:

- Is there something you want to commit to but are hesitating because it feels gigantic? What is it? Write it down here.
- What's your hesitation? Who can you talk with about this and then, with their guidance, make a decision to commit or not?
- Big or small, choose *one thing* you are going to commit to accomplish before year-end. What is the *one thing* that would make a significant difference in your life? Maybe it's a business achievement, a health commitment, or a relationship goal. Write it down here, and be sure to tell someone about it.

Notes and Thoughts

CHAPTER 27

LOOKING GOOD & FEELING GREAT

Not long ago, my client Rita made the decision to stop her cancer treatment. She had fought hard but had finally decided that enough was enough. She was in her late eighties, retired, and moved down South, and she was traveling up to Massachusetts one last time to say goodbye to her friends. I was grateful to be on the list of people she had chosen to visit.

She arrived at my office directly from the airport. I wasn't sure if she'd be able to walk upstairs, so I asked my team to keep her safely on the first floor. I was upstairs in my office preparing for what I knew would be our last meeting together. Rita had gone through more than a year of chemo, and it understandably had taken its toll on her.

I came downstairs to meet with her. When I walked into the conference room, I was not prepared for what I saw.

I was expecting a frail and pale old woman. There she was, a slightly smaller version of her old self, yet she looked radiant and wonderful! I was shocked by the person in front of me.

Rita was wearing a colorful floral shirt, a new white pair of pants, and trendy sandals. Her hair was perfect—it was almost impossible to know she was wearing a wig. Her lipstick sparkled pink and bright, and the color of her lips matched her manicured nails. I smiled and leaned in to hug her. When she returned the smile, I also couldn't help but notice her **beautiful new teeth**.

"Rita! You look amazing!" I went on to compliment her outfit and how fantastic she appeared. She was beaming with pride. We sat next to each other at the table, and she put her hand on top of mine. I asked her candidly how she was doing.

"I feel better ever since I stopped treatment. I know I'm not well, but I'm making the most of the time I have left." Then she went on to tell me that she had made it a priority to look her best for as long as possible because she wanted people to remember her this way.

She said it had all started when one of her grandsons showed her how to order clothes online. She had purchased several outfits with coordinating shoes. Her daughter made sure her hair looked great by helping her purchase fashionable wigs to cover her bald head.

And as for her teeth? Rita really wanted to buy new dentures to go with her new lease on life. She had always been a bit embarrassed by her smile and decided to go to her dentist to get a quote on fixing her teeth once and for all.

She found out that brand-new dentures—top and bottom—would cost her $8,000. She had a big decision to make and decided to have a heart-to-heart with herself about this large expense. She and her husband (who passed away a few years earlier) had worked very hard for their money. It had always been a priority in their planning to leave behind a legacy for their grown children. Rita weighed her desire to purchase new teeth with the realization that each of her four children would end up inheriting $2,000 less when she eventually passed.

She decided it was totally worth it!

She booked the appointment and made sure that the new dentures were put in place the week before her trip to Massachusetts.

Rita and I reviewed her financial plan together one last time. I told her how much I loved her, how proud I was of how boldly she lived in retirement, and how brave she was during her treatment. I told her that I admired her for prioritizing herself. She was beaming with confidence and happiness. You could see in her beautiful smile and in the way she carried herself that she felt like a million bucks.

After we said our goodbyes, Rita did what she had always done at the end of our meetings: She took the bowl of Hershey kisses in the middle of the conference room table and dumped the contents of the entire bowl into her purse. We laughed and hugged again. That was the last time I saw her. She passed away a few short months later back in Florida with her entire family by her side.

I think Rita is an incredible role model. She and her husband worked hard, saved money, planned for their future, and made smart decisions throughout retirement. They loved each other, adored their children and grandchildren, traveled the globe, and did just about everything they ever desired to do.

When her husband died, Rita kept traveling for as long as she was able. And despite a lifetime of adventures and having fun spending her hard-earned money, she was still able to leave behind a legacy for her family.

For some people, life is short. For others, life is long. Either way, all we have is the time we are allotted. Please do something terrific, both for yourself and for the people you love, with the precious time you have.

Ideas to Spark, Connect & Create this week:

- What could you do to take better care of yourself? Is it time to upgrade your eyeglasses, get new hearing aids, or buy a fun outfit, just because?

- Perhaps it is time to reach out and help your parents with upgrading some of these important items?

- What could you do to help an elderly person in your life feel better, have more confidence, and look spiffier in their appearance? A new pair of shoes, a colorful purse, or a trendy winter hat could make a difference in how someone feels about themselves. It doesn't take much. Do not overthink it—just do it.

- Do you have parents who are reluctant to spend their money because they are saving it for you? What if you encouraged them to spend it now? Consider they might simply need your blessing to take some action.

Notes and Thoughts

CHAPTER 28

APPARENTLY, GIRLS DRINK TEA

Dottie and June were sisters, had never married, and were still living in the house they grew up in when we met. They had worked for the same company for forty years and were finally both retiring. I had been referred to them by an employee from their company, a male coworker to whom they often turned for advice.

They needed help with retirement planning and called me for guidance.

In our very first meeting, we connected instantly. They welcomed me to their kitchen table and offered me a cup of tea. The pot was already steeping on the stove.

We sipped tea together as I asked them questions for the next ninety minutes. They were very forthcoming with their information and shared their goals were to roll over their 401(k) plans, understand their social security options, and determine if they should buy long-term care insurance.

The sisters were witty and sharp. I was excited to work with them on their financial plan.

A week later, I returned to their house. They preferred 3:00 p.m. meetings because they both took afternoon naps. My tea was already poured, and I took my seat at the kitchen table. I had spent a lot of time working on their plan and was excited to present what I thought were very straightforward recommendations.

Dottie asked the questions. June took the notes for the two of them. They both paid attention to the details and nodded during each recommendation as though it all made sense to them.

At the end of our meeting, they said they'd like to think about everything, and they asked me to come back the following week. I agreed.

I returned to their home for our third meeting. We proceeded to have the exact same conversation we had the week before. They confirmed they understood the reasons for my recommendations. They wanted to understand what the process would look like if they applied for long-term care insurance and how it would work to have me manage their investments. I walked them through all the forms and thoroughly answered all their questions. At the end of the meeting, they said they were not ready to fill out the paperwork and asked me to come back in a week.

I had three of these same meetings with no signs of implementation.

The following week, I brought this dilemma to my colleagues at our Monday morning planning meeting. I confidently presented the facts of the case, reviewed Dottie and June's goals, and shared all my recommendations. My colleagues nodded throughout my presentation as though they agreed with all of it.

I asked if anyone had any advice for me on how to encourage Dottie and June to move forward.

Andy was an advisor two years ahead of me in terms of experience, a bit arrogant, and spoke right up. "I'll tell you what your problem is: You're a girl."

I tried not to get immediately offended, but I was.

Andy saw my face and realized he needed to explain further.

"Look, Amy," he said, "this isn't a criticism. It's a fact. You're talking with two retired ladies who've never been married. They got referred to you by a man at work. Before that, they probably took advice from their father. They trust advice from men. They'll probably never take advice from you because you're a woman. And you're also too young for them to take your advice seriously."

I was both annoyed and intrigued. I kept listening.

"I'm so certain this is true," claimed Andy, "that I'd be willing to go to the next meeting and present the case exactly the way you did. How much do you want to bet they will move forward? I won't even share in the compensation with you. I just want to prove my point."

I was frustrated enough with my lack of success with these clients that I agreed to Andy's offer.

I called Dottie and June to let them know I'd be bringing my colleague Andy with me. They were happy to have him join me. Andy and I showed up at 3:00 p.m. and entered the kitchen. My cup of tea was in its place.

But there was no cup for Andy.

Instead, my clients shook his hand, thanked him for accompanying me to the appointment, and offered him a beer.

A beer.

We sat together at the table, me sipping my tea and Andy drinking his beer. I gave a brief overview of my recommendations, and then Dottie said she'd like to hear from my boss about what he thinks. **My boss**. Andy smiled warmly, told them that he had reviewed my recommendations, and he thought they were great.

He then reached out, put his hand on each of their hands across the table, and said, "If you were my grandmother, this is exactly what I would advise you to do."

And I kid you not, with no hesitation, Dottie and June immediately and enthusiastically agreed to move forward with all the paperwork. We completed the meeting in under thirty minutes—not ninety minutes, two cups of tea, and no action.

There was nothing Andy said in the meeting that I had not already said in all of my previous conversations with them.

Turns out, he was right.

This was a pivotal moment in my career. I would never have come to this same conclusion if Andy hadn't given me such direct feedback. Even though I was totally prepared for the meeting and clear in all my communication, *I failed to understand my audience.*

How often do we get caught up in our presentations, our recommendations, and our analyses—but fail to recognize that none of it matters if we do not know our audience?

In hindsight, I should have asked: Is there anyone you typically go to for advice regarding important financial decisions?

This was a humbling experience for me. To this day, I still appreciate my colleague Andy's insight. And I learned a valuable lesson: Sometimes, being humble can be more powerful than simply being knowledgeable.

Ideas to Spark, Connect & Create this week:

- Have you ever made a presentation you thought was excellent, only to find your audience disagreeing? Looking back, what could you have done differently to prepare? Did you *really* know your audience?
- Think about an upcoming opportunity where you are planning to present an idea or argument to someone (your child, your coworkers, or a

board of directors). What additional questions might you want to ask before you create your presentation? Putting your ego aside, would you come across as more compelling if you asked someone to present with you?

- Have you been on the receiving end of a less-than-compelling presentation? Did you offer any feedback to the presenter? What if you go back to offer it now? Imagine your candor could make all the difference for that person's effectiveness moving forward.

Notes and Thoughts

CHAPTER 29

WHEN I GROW UP

We have all heard a young person say, "When I grow up, I want to be a . . . " And then they enthusiastically share their career aspirations to be a professional singer, a veterinarian, an astronaut, or even a TikTok star.

For many of us, the career we have today can be traced back to something we were passionate about around age seven. Take my sister, Nicki, for example. When she was age seven, she used to spend hours in the basement in her "classroom." She'd line up her stuffed animals and dolls in rows, and they were her students. She had a chalkboard where she'd teach weekly lessons. When she wasn't playing school, Nicki could be found playing store. She'd set up her Fisher Price cash register on the kitchen counter and would pull canned goods and other food items from our cabinets, pretend to slide them down the conveyor belt, and manage her grocery checkout line. For a kid who loved teaching as well as counting money, it was no surprise that Nicki ended up with a double master's in mathematics and education. She became a high school math teacher and loved that job for the first decade of her career. We all could have predicted that was her path!

What many of us were passionate about when we were age seven often shapes who we become later in life. Take me as another example. (Disclaimer: I was a weird kid.)

When I was seven, I discovered my love of money. I was an entrepreneur from the start. And I also loved selling things. My grandmother showed me how to crochet when I was in kindergarten, and I'd spend hours following simple patterns she taught me. I quickly learned how to make little crocheted hearts, shamrocks, and Easter bunnies that you'd pin on your coat for the holidays. I crocheted everywhere and anywhere. And grown-ups were so intrigued that a young person could make such items they often asked if they could buy them from me.

This is how I started my first business.

I ramped up my crocheting in the winter months to get my inventory prepared. My mom would loan me money at the beginning of every season for my supplies. I bought the yarn, ribbon, googly eyes, glue, and safety pins from the local craft store. Then I'd get my assembly line set up.

Easter was a particularly busy season for me. I'd crochet all the Easter bunnies early in March. I would also make little bows for their necks with pastel ribbons, carefully add the safety pins on the back of each, and finally glue on the eyes. Once I had dozens and dozens of my finished products ready, I would fill up my Easter basket and go door-to-door in my neighborhood selling my goods.

Any leftovers I had, I brought to church on Sundays and sold them to all the ladies in the pews around me before mass got started.

I made enough money every season to pay my mom back my microloan and then use my profits to buy something I was saving up for. From as far back as I can remember, I understood money, knew how to manage it, and loved having cash in my wallet.

I also thought this was what all kids learned from their parents.

My dad continued teaching us about saving. When I was in eighth grade, my parents brought me to the bank to open my own checking account. They made me feel really special—fancy even—going through this process. My sister and I were encouraged to deposit birthday and holiday gifts into our checking accounts. We were shown how to save up for the things we wanted. We were also taught how to balance a checkbook register to the penny. I genuinely loved this activity! When the monthly bank statement arrived in the mail with my name on it, I knew what my evening plan was going to be. Back then, this seemed totally normal to me, and I again assumed it was what other kids were doing. I had no idea how unusual this ritual was for a kid. I most definitely didn't know that these important money lessons would shape my future career choice.

Dad also set up small stock portfolios for Nicki and me. Each Sunday, he would show us how to look up our shares in the finance section of the newspaper to see if the values had gone up or down (Reminder: This was in the '80s, pre-internet). It was a highlight of my weekend as a young child to look up my stocks, see how much I had made or lost that week, think about money, and save and plan for things I wanted. (As I mentioned, I was a weird kid.)

In hindsight, *of course* I found myself drawn to a career in financial services. I love teaching people about money. I love helping them save and achieve goals. Eventually, I launched my own financial planning firm and built a team of advisors and staff who felt passionate about the work too.

My desire to be an entrepreneur began at age seven. By the time I was twenty-five, I already had almost twenty years of training, coaching, risk-taking, and knowing how to profitably run a start-up!

As I look back at my childhood, I'm grateful that my parents took the time to share these fundamental lessons with my sister and me at such a young age. What started as an enjoyable hobby as a kid turned into my life's work.

To this day, I love helping families manage their money, create wealth for future generations, and build meaningful legacies. My sister (the math major and former high school teacher) is now the bookkeeper of our firm. Together we are both doing a more sophisticated version of the things we were passionate about forty-plus years ago.

I share this with all you future parents, current parents, grandparents, coaches, and teachers as a reminder. The lessons you teach children today can influence them far greater than you might realize tomorrow.

Take time to share important concepts you're familiar with and passionate about. Expose children to hobbies and adventures and help them connect with the things that spark joy in their young minds.

You never know when the time you spend building structures out of LEGO sets could eventually create a future architect or the time playing Minecraft turns out to be an investment in a future computer programmer.

Teach what you know, encourage kids to try unfamiliar things, and demonstrate as many great ideas as you can while they are young. Never underestimate the impact of those early lessons. Your influence matters.

And if you happen to have a young child or grandchild who is great with money, send them to me in twenty years. I'd like to interview them for a future career opportunity!

Ideas to Spark, Connect & Create this week:

- What skill, craft, or hobby are you awesome at? Are you teaching this to anyone? Would you enjoy sharing this skill with a young person in your life? Who?
- Think back to when you were six or seven years old. What were you doing back then that made you happy? Are you doing that—or something similar—now? If not, is it time to reconnect with that old passion of yours? What would it take to do that?
- Is there a teacher, coach, mentor, or family member who profoundly impacted your life because of the skill they taught you? Have you recently thanked them for it? Plan to do this in the next week.

Notes and Thoughts

CHAPTER 30

BREAKFAST SANDWICH TO-GO

My friend Payton just finished celebrating her annual "Mama Days." She has three children. Every year she takes three days off from work and dedicates an entire day to each of her kids. From the moment they wake up in the morning until the day is done, each of the kids gets to choose what he or she wants to do, all day, just with Mom (similar to Jennifer Garner's movie, *Yes Day*).

Payton commemorates the days' events by posting the most heartfelt pictures and stories on social media about their adventures—from the zoo to pedicures to virtual-reality gaming adventures. Each child, unique in his or her own way, chooses completely different activities from their siblings. You can imagine this takes tremendous dedication and commitment on Mom's part to follow through with this tradition every year. She wouldn't miss it and claims the kids look as forward to their Mama Days as they do Christmas morning.

My friend Jack has an eighty-nine-year-old mother. Although his life is busy running his company and spending time with his young grandkids, he dedicates every Sunday morning to his mother. Since she no longer drives, he picks her up at 8:30 a.m. and takes her across town to church for 9:00 a.m. mass. They sit in the same pew every week. He helps his mom through all the rituals, walks with her to the front of the church to receive communion, and safely gets her back to the car. Then they go to McDonald's for her favorite breakfast: a bacon, egg, and cheese biscuit, hash browns, and a small coffee. She loves going to the drive-thru and having a "car picnic" in the parking lot with her breakfast sandwich to-go. She looks forward to one-on-one time with her son and calls him an angel for consistently doing this with her.

Aunt Alice lives in Florida. Most of her family lives in Connecticut, including Emily, her youngest niece. Emily is working on her master's degree in education, teaching part-time in a local elementary school, and has a busy life. She makes time, however, to call Aunt Alice once a week on her commute to work. Each Monday at 7:10 a.m., Emily shares lesson plans and ideas she has for the students, and Aunt Alice always offers ideas and opinions. For Emily, it's an easy ten-minute call to her favorite auntie.

And Aunt Alice will tell you it is most certainly the highlight of her week.

What kinds of traditions do you keep in place for other people? Do you carve out time each month for your great-grandfather in the nursing home or bring your elderly uncle to the cemetery so he can "visit" with his wife, who died years ago?

What small effort do you continue to make on a regular basis that makes a big difference for someone else?

I started a tradition in high school for my favorite teacher, Sister Catherine. She was a big fan of the seasonal ice cream Jubilee Roll from Friendly's. This holiday treat only came out during the Christmas season. I used to bring one to her every year when school got out for Christmas break. And for years after graduation, when I was home from college, I'd take a ride to Friendly's and drop off a Jubilee Roll at the convent where Sr. Catherine lived. It was a small errand for me, but it was so special for her and her friends.

Although a retired hairdresser, my mom continues to make house calls to a small group of elderly clients who are homebound. Mom calls it "no big deal," but to the clients who are looking spiffy after Mom's visit, **it's a very big deal**. I'd even call it a confetti moment.

What could you do that would be a small effort for you yet make a big impact on someone else?

Isn't this what life is all about—making the extra effort to share joy, happiness, and kindness?

Ideas to Spark, Connect & Create this week:

- Is there someone you can reach out to who might not have the freedom, flexibility, or mobility you have? What could you offer to help them do this week?
- Is there a child who could use some individual attention from you?
- Is there someone who'd appreciate a breakfast sandwich to-go and a chance to spend an occasional Sunday morning with you?
- Make this the week you carve out time for those special people and get them on your calendar. Who immediately comes to mind?

Notes and Thoughts

CHAPTER 31

TURN DOWN FOR WHAT?

I recently returned from a trip to Toronto, where I attended a quarterly coaching session for entrepreneurs. I had been part of this group for the past four years, and I would fly to Toronto every quarter to attend in person. Then the pandemic hit, and we went virtual for two years. Sure, being on Zoom has been easier, more convenient, a time-saver, and avoids the risks and potential inconveniences of international travel.

But nothing compares to being there in person.

When I arrived on Sunday, I checked into my hotel. I always stay at the Ritz Carlton. I am aware that it is a total splurge to do this. The place is beautiful and modern and features the most spectacular fresh floral displays at the entrance.

In the lobby, I am greeted warmly by every worker I pass by. When I approach the reception desk, I am welcomed to the hotel by a friendly man with a perfect

French accent. He asks if I'd like a bottle of water. I answer yes. He further inquires if I want it chilled or room temperature. I confirm chilled.

I can see behind the desk that there is a refrigerator filled with cold bottles of water, as well as a basket filled with the same bottles but room temp. The man removes a bottle from the fridge, walks out from behind his desk, and comes over to hand it to me personally.

Their service is thoughtful and impeccable. **Always**.

When I get to my room, it's only 2:00 p.m., and dinner with my friends isn't until 6:00 p.m. One of my favorite hotel luxuries is room service. I pick up the phone and order a tuna poke bowl, one of their signature dishes. The woman who answers my call tells me that my lunch will arrive within twenty to twenty-five minutes. I look at my watch and note the time.

Exactly twenty-one minutes later, there's a knock at my door. A man delivers a tray carrying the most beautiful poke bowl I've ever seen. And next to it is a tiny ceramic pot with a purple orchid. When the man exits my room, I feel compelled to touch a leaf.

It's real.

The attention to detail at this hotel makes me feel so welcome. It's like a homecoming of comfort and luxury and familiarity. After two years of being away, I am so pleased that my hotel experience is exactly like I remembered (and hoped) it would still be.

My friends and I meet up a few hours later for dinner. We have a terrific time catching up and reconnecting, and we agree that we've been on Zoom for far too long.

I walk back to my hotel, and as the bellman opens the door for me, I'm greeted by the most divine smell. I cannot pinpoint the exact ingredients it consists of, but I can tell you that it's definitely the scent of a superior hotel. Again, I am filled with a feeling of coziness and comfort, like being home. (*To be clear, my home doesn't smell like this—that would be amazing. But if you know where I can buy the Ritz Carlton scent, please call me.*)

When I return to my room, I hear spa-like music playing. It's coming from the television. All my lights are dimmed. The curtains are drawn for the night, and my bed is turned down. There is a fresh bottle of water on the nightstand and a simple square of dark chocolate wrapped in gold foil next to it.

Turn-down service.

This is the one thing I appreciate even more than room service. Very few hotels do this anymore. For the record, it's completely unnecessary, totally luxurious.

And I absolutely love it.

I find myself smiling, alone in my tranquil and dim room, wondering **what it is about this that makes me so happy**.

To me, turn-down service evokes that feeling of being tucked into bed as a child by a parent. It's as if someone wants to make certain every detail is being prepared for my slumber, that I feel safe and comfy under my covers, and that my nightlight is adjusted just right. Do you know that feeling?

That, for me, is turn-down service.

I have been reflecting on this luxury hotel experience over the past several weeks since my return from Toronto. It has inspired me to also increase my awareness of customer service details.

For example, at our office, I always want to be sure we have thoughtful amenities for clients who are coming to meet me in person. That means offering great tea and coffee choices, providing almond milk in addition to half-and-half, leaving chocolate treats in little bowls upstairs and down, as well as a collection of healthy Kind Bars and packets of cashews if anyone needs a snack during our meeting.

We also keep a tray on the conference room table with paper, nice pens, colorful Post-its and highlighters, and always extra reading glasses.

You might be asking yourself, *Do these details really matter*?

Last week, a new client came in and commented on how much she loved our pens. I put five more on the table. She happily tucked them all into her purse to take them home.

The details matter.

But the thing is, we never know **which** details and **to whom**—so we must assume that they all matter and tend to our people with this as a priority.

The best financial advisors give their clients "Ritz-Carlton-like" experiences. And I do not mean that you need to provide pricey amenities. I mean that in working with you, your clients immediately feel a sense of warmth and safety and comfort because of the details you've thought of and because of the experience you have curated for them.

Maybe it's the personal note you send in the mail acknowledging that your client's last child is off to college, and you know the empty-nester adjustment can be difficult.

Maybe it's the time you pause on a Zoom call to notice the photographs hanging on your client's wall—giraffes and zebras—and she smiles and takes the next five minutes to reminisce about her trip to Africa and the life-changing safari she got to experience with her husband before he passed away.

These simple details matter. They demonstrate that you are listening, that you are paying attention.

What are you doing each day to ensure that the people around you feel special and cared for?

Did your mom ever put a little love note in your lunchbox as a kid? What if you left one on the kitchen counter for your spouse, a simple note of encouragement to kickstart his or her week?

When was the last time you Venmo-ed your assistant over the weekend with the message that dinner for her and her husband was on you?

What could you do to demonstrate to your colleagues, your spouse—heck, even your mom—how much you care?

Turn-down service: It is completely unnecessary, totally luxurious, **and feels wonderful**.

Who doesn't want a little of *that* every once in a while? Why don't you be the one to make it happen for someone?

Ideas to Spark, Connect & Create this week:

- Your theme this week is to spread the love! Who are the five people you are going to reach out to, do something special for, drop a love note in the mail to, or create a turn-down-like feeling for? Write their names down.
- Now identify what it is you're going to do for each of these five important people.

Notes and Thoughts

CHAPTER 32

WHATEVER FLOATS YOUR BOAT

Over the weekend, we gathered a small group of friends and family for a boat-naming ceremony. When you buy a new boat, there is a tradition you are supposed to follow to properly name it:

1. Bring together a group of friends.
2. Officially announce your boat's name and share a few words explaining its meaning.
3. Ask for the gods of the sea (or, in our case, the river) to watch over your boat and your passengers.
4. Break a bottle of (not too good) champagne alongside your boat and pour it over the name.

If you choose to rename a boat that was previously owned by someone else, you follow the same tradition by thanking the boat for the past, welcoming its new future, and officially replacing the old name with the new.

At the end of 2020, we sold our pontoon boat (named *The Satellite Office*) to a nice young couple who were so excited to have a boat of their own. We ordered ourselves a newer, faster boat which got delivered at the beginning of the 2021 boating season. This was the beginning of our tenth year as boaters. Prior to that, we had spent our summers golfing, vacationing on Cape Cod, and enjoying backyard BBQs.

But once we got our first boat, all those old traditions were replaced with new ones: long Saturdays floating on the river, tying up our boats to our friends' boats to create a giant flotilla, chasing the sunsets, and enjoying a crisp glass of white wine as the evenings came to a close.

In fact, we haven't golfed, been to the Cape, or hosted a backyard BBQ in ten years. Every day is simply spent enjoying the simplicity, the repetition, and the calm of the river.

As we were prepping for our boat-naming ceremony, it occurred to me how special our boating traditions are to us. Typically, we boat from May until September. If the river cooperates, sometimes our season can stretch all the way into October.

The transformation along the riverbank each May is exciting to watch. In April, there are no docks nor any boats in the water. Over the course of a few weekends, groups of hardworking people help re-anchor all the docks into place. Then the pickup trucks and trailers arrive at the marina as families one by one launch their boats back into the water for another season.

Friends we haven't seen all winter emerge from hibernation, pale and ready for sunshine, sporting bathing suits, baseball caps, and boat shoes.

There is a cadence to our activities: We plan our weekends around the weather, who's coming out with us for the afternoon, and what to pack for the day. There's casual coordination among our friends. This tradition repeats every summer as we unplug from our busy workdays to simply enjoy the water.

On a sunny Sunday afternoon in May, we gathered with friends and family, popped open a very cheap bottle of champagne, and announced the name of our boat: *Two Chicks on Board*. This was an ironic spinoff of the acronym TCOB which usually stands for Takin' Care of Business. As I poured the champagne across the colorful lettering alongside the back of the boat, Kim popped open a much better bottle and shared it with all our boating friends who were gathered for our ceremony.

The boating season had officially begun.

The following weekend, we were out on our boat sipping coffee and enjoying another sunny Saturday morning. Several docks over from where we were anchored, we recognized our old boat. The new owners were gathered with a group of people on their dock and conducted the same ceremony with their friends. They retired our *Satellite Office* and gave their boat its new name, commemorating her late father's love of the river.

It struck me how important and meaningful it is to continue old traditions and to also welcome new beginnings.

As we make the change from spring to summer, what are your change-of-season traditions? What does your family do at this time of the year that you are excited about?

Will you spend the weekend planting flowers in your flower boxes, staking your tomato plants, getting your grass seeded and your in-ground sprinkler system turned on?

Are you helping plan a graduation, prep for prom, or address wedding invitations? Did you dust off your convertible to get it ready for a season of sunshine? Are you buying tickets for a summer concert to see your favorite band play?

Whatever your traditions are at the change of each season, I hope you will welcome them with appreciation and gratitude and invite all the people who are most important to you to join in your confetti moments.

Ideas to Spark, Connect & Create this week:

- What are your favorite traditions? Are there any that you used to love but haven't done in a while?
- What is a tradition from the past that you could bring back to life? Gathering the whole family for Grandpa's birthday? Getting your Polish aunts

together to make pierogi before the holidays? Getting the neighborhood together for a Fourth of July block party? Write down something that you used to love doing, you've missed, and you're committed to bringing back.

- What's a tradition you could start? What if you kicked off the first annual Ridge Road progressive dinner party? Or hosted a pumpkin carving contest for the whole family? Maybe you're going to be the catalyst for a new book club, an office poker tournament, or a trivia night. Write down a new idea that you could create and could eventually turn into an old tradition because of your efforts.

- Thinking about buying a pontoon boat? I highly recommend it!

Notes and Thoughts

CHAPTER 33

THE POWER OF HAVING FOUR WINGS

The dragonfly is an amazing creature.

With four wings, dragonflies have twenty times more power than any other insect. They can move in all six directions. They can hover like a helicopter, fly backward, move straight up and down, and even fly from side-to-side. Flying forward, they can go up to forty-five miles per hour. There are more than 3,000 species of dragonflies still in existence, and they have been around since prehistoric times.

Dragonflies spend the first part of their life in a cocoon-like state as they grow and develop. Then they eventually emerge, colorful and agile, each one unique.

In terms of their symbolism, dragonflies are said to represent change, transformation, and new beginnings. Some even believe that the appearance of a dragonfly in your life indicates you are on the right track and that positive transformation is on the horizon.

I have carried this notion with me for more than twenty years now.

My father passed away in 1998. The day of his funeral, a dragonfly landed on my shoulder at the cemetery and stayed there for an hour. Dragonflies have reappeared dozens and dozens of other times for me, and in the most unexpected places: on my windshield in the middle of winter and even on an airplane window. The dragonfly showed up exactly at the same time the pilot announced we were experiencing some technical difficulties, but not to worry. We then sat on the tarmac for twenty minutes until the problem was fixed. That dragonfly remained on the outside of my airplane window the entire time. When the pilot announced that the problem had been resolved and we would be on our way, I watched the dragonfly finally fly away.

Each time this little creature has appeared to me, I take comfort in the idea that maybe it's somehow my dad coming for a visit.

I recently started comparing our pre- and post-pandemic lives to the life cycle of a dragonfly. Think about it. Most of us lived in a cocoon-like state from March 2020 until mid-2021. It was quite a long and drawn-out fifteen months of slow growth. Then we all began to slowly re-emerge—many of us nimbler and more resilient than before.

What a feeling of freedom it was to finally be able to move in so many directions! We shifted from doing

nothing to being able to do just about **anything**. We can now hop on a plane and fly in almost any direction. We can go to a baseball game and enjoy seeing the stands at full capacity. We can hug our families, celebrate holidays in person, and not live with the fears and insecurities many of us felt in 2020.

The next time you see a dragonfly, take a closer look. Notice the way it flies and its ability to move in all six directions. Does this feel at all familiar to you? Maybe you are someone who's **hovering in place right now**, trying to decide in which direction you should be moving. Maybe you are someone who has been **flying in the wrong direction**—perhaps even backward—and now you need to figure out how to gain forward momentum again. You might be someone who has had the fortune of **flying straight up**, experiencing unprecedented growth and success recently. Maybe it's time to pause and ask yourself: Where do you go from here?

I like the idea that the dragonfly is a special symbol that seems to show up at just the right time. What if this is true for you too? No matter where you happen to be right now, trust that you are on the right track. Let us assume positive transformation is on the horizon, and we can all fly in any direction we choose.

Ideas to Spark, Connect & Create this week:

- Where are you currently stuck? In what area of your life are you experiencing zero forward momentum? Work? Home? Marriage? Write it down.
- Is there someone you currently blame for this issue? Is there a particular person or a circumstance contributing to this feeling of being stuck? Write that down too.
- Now pause for a moment, take a deep breath, and assume that you are 100 percent responsible for being stuck. If you put all blame aside and assume no one else is to blame for this current status, what is one small step you could take to move this issue forward or get past it? Write it down.
- As you write, are there other brilliant ideas your brain is suddenly filled with that could propel you forward? You don't need to tackle them all at once. Do, however, take the time to write them down here. Use this as your inspiration and your future to-do list.

Notes and Thoughts

CHAPTER 34

WHEN EIGHT OARS ARE IN SYNC

During my first year at Middlebury College, I signed up for the crew team. By "signed up," I mean there were no tryouts. It was a club sport started by a very charismatic student named Phil. Unbeknownst to his parents, Phil showed up for college and immediately sold the brand-new Macintosh computer they had bought for him. Instead, he used the money to purchase the basic equipment needed to get the crew team started.

With $1200, Phil bought two old wooden boats and finagled a friend at Vassar to donate sixteen used wooden oars.

Twenty-four of us signed up for the crew team that fall. We were enamored by Phil. Under his leadership, we spent a weekend painting the oars with black and white cow spots. Then we carried the boats on our shoulders to the shore of Lake Dunmore to officially begin the rowing season.

Apparently, I was outspoken during our first practice. As a result, Phil appointed me the coxswain for the men's eight. That meant my job was to sit at the front of the boat facing my eight rowers and shout commands at them to keep their strokes synchronized. I had no prior experience but was excited to learn.

In crew, when all eight oars sync up, a boat glides so swiftly and smoothly across the water—it's magical to watch from the shore. It is even more incredible to witness this moment from the boat itself.

Normally the cox has a battery-operated headset, and boats come equipped with small speakers so that even the rower at the very back can hear each command clearly.

Such was not the case for us.

Before climbing into the boat for the first time, I was handed a small megaphone (think plastic cone with a string to wear around my neck as a small child might do). I was also given a bucket with a handle and a roll of heavy-duty duct tape.

I learned quickly that an important part of my job was duct-taping the cracks in the bottom of the boat before practice started. I took this job seriously. If water seeped into the boat, it made it so much heavier to move forward. The rowers needed me to do my part to avoid this from happening.

Once we were underway, the water would slowly start to make its way into the bottom of the boat. Whether it was from poor rowing, splashing, or the occasional morning rainstorm, I would also need to scoop water out with my bucket. As the rowers slid back in their seats to take a stroke, their backward movement created enough space in front of me to lean forward with my bucket and bail out as much water as I could before they slid forward again.

It was quite a scene.

We practiced at 5:00 a.m. on a cold lake in Vermont. The boat took on water every single time. This was unpleasant—not to mention making us significantly heavier and slower than the competition. When we traveled to regattas on weekends, it was embarrassing to unload our old boats and cow-spotted oars alongside other schools who were fully equipped with trucks and shells, paid coaches, coordinated uniforms, shiny new equipment, and speed.

We were a wildly competitive bunch of rowers, but given the circumstances, it was nearly impossible to win a regatta in those early years.

Losing race after race, despite our efforts, was discouraging.

We continued to work hard all season. My rowers became more coachable. I became more educated about the sport. I learned each of my guys' idiosyncrasies and skills. Week after week, their blisters would reopen and bleed after every sprint. Despite the pain and the obstacles, we kept on trying.

We practiced the same drills every day alongside setbacks, leaks, and the bitter cold. It eventually came together, one slow stroke at a time.

By senior year, our college had recognized our collective efforts (and Phil's initial investment) and finally made the decision to provide full funding for our crew team. We became a sport instead of a club. Our old wooden boats were replaced by lightweight fiberglass shells. My duct tape, plastic megaphone, and bucket could be retired.

In fact, our men's and women's crew team finally found itself at the Head of the Charles in Boston, respectably competing against other elite New England schools by the time I graduated.

As I reminisce about my old crew days, I realize that my rowing experience was strikingly similar to my experience as a new financial advisor. In the beginning of my career, I didn't have the skills, nor was I equipped to do my job well. Every day offered me new opportunities to practice, develop, learn, and get better. On particularly challenging days when clients canceled appointments, or they didn't take my recommendations, or they stood me up altogether, I'd need the proverbial duct tape to patch myself together.

Think about the last time you started a new career or tried to learn a brand-new skill. You probably had very few wins in the beginning. Everyone else with experience appears to be more professional, is equipped with better tools, and may even cruise right past you in their success. While you are struggling, they make the work look easy.

Do you remember starting something brand-new and how awkward and challenging it was?

Do you also recall the point where it all began to come together? Your new skills start to sync up. Your processes become less awkward, and you become more confident. In due time, you begin to glide in a faster and more polished way.

Maybe eventually, you'll even build and develop a team. As the leader, it's your job to help everyone move in the right direction, guiding and steering them along the way. Hopefully, you find that your team learns to pull for you too. They get better because of your leadership, your vision, and your consistent coaching.

It may take *years*, but when each person's individual skills synchronize with their teammates, our work becomes easier, our blisters turn to callouses, the pain subsides, and we all get exponentially stronger and faster together.

Ideas to Spark, Connect & Create this week:

- When was the last time you experienced true teamwork? What characteristics or attributes were present? What was the leader like? What did it feel like to be on a winning team (at work, at home, in your community)?

- Maybe you are on a team that is currently lacking leadership or cohesion. What could you do to change that dynamic?
- If you're the leader, what needs to shift in terms of your approach?
- If you're not the leader, is there any advice or feedback you could give the group that might make a difference?
- When was the last time you tried something totally new, with no experience at all? What if you signed up for a painting class, learned to play pickleball, or asked your grandchild to teach you something new about technology?

Notes and Thoughts

CHAPTER 35

WHICH DO YOU PREFER?

"Do you prefer rainbow sprinkles or chocolate sprinkles?" I asked.

"Definitely rainbow sprinkles!"

My son, who was six at the time, answered my question with excitement. Then he launched right into asking his own version of the question. "Mom, which do you prefer: ice cream or pizza?"

"Definitely pizza. You know there isn't much else I'd choose over pizza!"

When our kids were little, we often played the game, "Which Do You Prefer?" It was an easy way to engage in conversation as a family, distract the kids at the dinner table, and give them a chance to equally participate in the back-and-forth discussion. We played this game all the time.

In the beginning, the questions were simple, like which do you prefer: strawberries or bananas? Then the kids started getting creative: "Which do you prefer, a ski vacation in a snowy place in the mountains with your best friend or a tropical vacation in the sunshine on a cruise ship with just the two of you?" The more detail they would add to their description of the choices, the tougher it became to answer the questions.

The game always included two options—that was the rule—and you had to pick which of the two options you preferred. "Both" was not an acceptable answer. The game challenged us all to think. And it is not overly challenging to choose between two things.

But that's not usually how life presents itself.

Often, we have far more than two options in front of us. This is a common occurrence. How often have you turned on your TV only to find yourself scrolling through hundreds if not thousands of movie choices? Do you find yourself so overwhelmed with suggestions that you end up shutting off the TV altogether?

This is called decision fatigue.

Decision fatigue is that overwhelming feeling you get when faced with too many choices. You end up paralyzed and unable to pick just one. Or even worse, you pick too many. Just envision any aisle in the grocery store and the dozens of options you have for ice cream, peanut butter, or cat litter. Have you ever tossed three pints of ice cream into your cart, telling yourself you'll make a choice when you get home about which you'd prefer?

Decision fatigue can be a real problem. And it's important to know scientifically that decision fatigue gets worse as the day goes on. Early in the morning, your brain is fresh and clear and has an easier time making decisions. For example: Do you find it easier to decide what to eat for breakfast versus dinner? That is because your brain is clearer about what it wants—and has fewer choices to consider—earlier in the day.

By the time you get to work, you are already slammed with tasks and emails and responsibilities in the first hour of your day. It can be difficult to sort out your options and decide which of these demands to tackle first. And the need to make decisions gets exponentially harder as the day goes on.

For some people, decision fatigue keeps them from making progress in life. They get stuck in "analysis paralysis" and cannot move forward. I've seen this show up in young people as well as retirees. Both age groups tend to have a lot of unstructured time. Too many choices lead to indecision—sometimes even total shutdown.

Bad news: You cannot avoid decision fatigue.

Good news: It is possible to manage it.

According to research, we can make as many as 35,000 decisions a day! Our choices are never as simple as rainbow sprinkles versus chocolate sprinkles. But we **can better equip ourselves** by narrowing down our options, preparing in advance for the week ahead, and tackling the tough stuff earlier in the day.

Which do you prefer: being bogged down with decision fatigue or being organized and prepared for the day ahead? It takes practice to continue choosing the latter.

Ideas to Spark, Connect & Create this week:

Take a look at your calendar for the next two weeks, then try out some of these techniques and tips:

- Make decisions **for next weekend** early in the week, when you are thinking more clearly.
- Make decisions **about today** earlier in the morning rather than later when you are likely to be tired.
- Preplan food for the week as much as possible. Grocery shop for specific meals instead of buying a bunch of random items. Pack your lunches and snacks in simple to-go containers. This prep can be so much easier on a Sunday because it's earlier in the week.
- Map out your day and write it all down on a calendar. Put tasks on your calendar at a specific time. You will start to create a sense of clarity and purpose for each day when you do this.
- Can't make a decision because you have too many options? Try the "Which Do You Prefer?" game with yourself! Pick two options and ask

yourself which of the two choices you prefer (getting your emails cleaned up or making that difficult phone call). Then take the winner of those two options and do it again. Narrow your decisions down, two at a time, and continue to choose the one you'd prefer. Repeat, repeat, repeat.

Notes and Thoughts

CHAPTER 36

WHAT OUR SCARS SAY

We recently had a successful photo shoot at our office. The updated pictures of everyone came out great, and I was excited to add them to our website once the final proofs were done. The photographer emailed us the album of all the shots. She asked us to look them over carefully and let her know if there were any extra touch-ups any of us wanted.

"Yes, would you mind covering up the scar on my face a little more? The one under my right eye." My request seemed straightforward.

The photographer seemed surprised. "What scar? I don't see anything under your eye."

How could she not see it? That faint line down my right cheek was all I could see when I looked at my photo.

Granted, it's been five years, and my face has had plenty of time to heal. I follow a makeup technique each morning that mostly covers what's left of the evidence of my surgery. And you probably would not notice it if I didn't point it out to you. But I still see it.

Five years ago, I had a tiny pimple under my right eye that would not go away. My dermatologist didn't like the look of it during my routine check-up and decided to do a biopsy.

Thank goodness she did.

Turns out I had a precancerous tumor hiding under that little bump and needed to have it removed immediately. To successfully accomplish this, it took a dermatological surgeon, then an ocular plastic surgeon, to carefully get rid of the olive-sized tumor, make sure they didn't damage my eye or my tear duct in the process, and repair the damage.

I was left with 100 stitches on my face and twelve weeks of recovery.

I am fine now. The recovery went better than expected. I have no residual cancer. But every time I look in the mirror, the faint scar all the way down my cheek is the first thing I notice. On Zoom calls—when the sun comes through the window and hits my face at just the wrong angle—I move my camera in an attempt to hide it.

Do you have scars you try to hide?

Do your scars tell a story about you and your past? For me, they do. There's the skinned knee I got in second grade that never quite healed but reminds me that I was running with excitement to my best friend's house when it happened. I have my C-section scar, a reminder that my baby, who was born a preemie, will turn twenty-two next year.

We all have scars that originated somewhere in our past and likely will remain with us for our lifetimes.

Wouldn't you agree that each one is a part of who we are?

Some people's scars are visible to everyone. Others have scars that are easy to hide with clothing or makeup, like those tiny incisions from your laparoscopic appendectomy or the very-bad-idea tattoo you eventually had removed with that painful laser procedure.

Other people carry the kind of scars that are invisible, the ones that tell a story of their past but are impossible for the rest of us to see. They might be the only one who knows they are there. These invisible scars, too, have in some way shaped who they have become.

Take a moment this week to think about your scars and what they say about you. Are you so accustomed to having them that you have forgotten to notice their presence? Or, like me, do you sometimes give them more weight than they need?

Maybe this is the week we take time to acknowledge our history and the scars we carry, both visible and invisible.

Let us trust that we are all stronger and braver because of them.

Ideas to Spark, Connect & Create this week:

- Take a moment to reminisce about the physical scars you have and where they came from. Does thinking about it take you right back to that moment: sliding into home plate and skinning both knees? Reflect on your scars and what you remember about them. What story do they each tell about you?

- Take a moment to think about your invisible scars, the ones only you can "see." Are you giving those old scars too much weight or merit? If the stories still serve you, then keep them. But if those old stories evoke bad feelings and prevent you from moving forward, maybe it's time to let them go.

Notes and Thoughts

CHAPTER 37

THE GIFT OF A LIFETIME

My client Joseph was approaching his eighty-eighth birthday. His wife and caregiver had passed away suddenly the year before. Initially, he had a tough time adjusting to living alone and having to ask others for help. Over time, he slowly started to build a routine and find his groove. He figured out integrating more technology into his life to make communication easier. He upgraded his laptop and his smartphone to newer versions. This allowed him to chat regularly with the family by emailing, texting, and even hopping on an occasional Zoom call.

One challenge he faced was the fact that he no longer drove a car. In fact, after his wife passed away, the family helped him sell her car. This meant that he had to find a new way of transportation to get to the senior center—his home away from home. He knew he could call their van, but it wasn't reliable and didn't exactly fit his regimented schedule.

Instead, he asked his kids for help. They downloaded the Uber app on his phone for him and connected it to his credit card. After a few practice runs, Joseph learned how to confidently summon an Uber when it was convenient for him and get wherever he needed to go. The beauty of living in a smallish town was that there were not many Uber drivers—which meant that, before long, they all knew Joseph and his usual drop-offs.

He figured out a new routine. He got reconnected to his community of friends at the senior center. He received help from a family member to get his bills paid each Saturday.

Once all those things were in place, he was able to start thinking about his legacy.

We met at his home early on a sunny summer afternoon. I offered a virtual meeting, but Joseph wanted a visit in person because he had important things to discuss.

Joseph was impressively prepared for our meeting. He had created and printed out a document outlining his end-of-life wishes. He gave me a copy and asked me to read it at that moment before we began our discussion. His letter was both thoughtful and thorough.

In it, he outlined all of his assets as well as his beneficiary intentions and charitable wishes. Specifically, he wanted to leave money to three charities, as well as give gifts to his four grandchildren at his passing. His words were clear and specific. He understood what he owned, who he cared about the most, and what his legacy would be once his wishes were carried out.

After we reviewed his letter together, he took me for a stroll around his living room. He pointed out his collectibles, a few antiques, and other sentimental items he had made a list of, specifying to whom they would be left. He was proud of each item and shared some fascinating stories with me about many of them. It was not a sad conversation—it was like a pleasant stroll down memory lane.

I absolutely loved our meeting. In fact, it was one of my favorites of the past twenty-five years.

It was so meaningful.

Certainly, it was a priority for Joseph to share his thoughts and ideas with someone "neutral," a financial advisor who could offer an outsider's perspective. He spent time reminiscing about his wife (who was a force to be reckoned with and whose very unexpected death profoundly affected his entire family). Joseph shared many stories about the past. We cried together. He ultimately reached some very important decisions by the end of our conversation.

As we were wrapping up, I had to ask, "Are you sure you want to wait until you are no longer here to make these gifts? Would you prefer to do this in your lifetime?"

"What do you mean?" he asked.

"Well, you are so clear about these gifts, and you care so much about the grandkids, your alma mater, and the senior center. Would you prefer to give these gifts to everyone **now**? While you are alive and well and able to experience the impact of these gifts **with them**?"

Joseph needed time to think about this.

He reached back out to me two weeks later to share his conclusion: Yes, he wanted to take care of this in his lifetime.

He was also inspired to write a personal letter of intent to each of the grandkids. He took the necessary time to craft each letter with thoughtfulness as only he could.

Joseph gathered with his family on Thanksgiving. They had a small and simple dinner. Afterward, he sat with the grandkids—all in their twenties—and handed them each a letter. The four messages were each unique.

I was so grateful when he emailed me afterward and shared an example. He also gave me permission to share it with you:

Dear Grandson,

In case I have not said this enough, you should know that since the day you were born, you have given great joy to Gram and to me. That joy has been, and is, priceless and would be impossible to match. Your fight for respect for all, especially for the challenged, is just one of your many qualities that have given us pride in you, as well as great delight. We hope you will allow us to make a gesture—a token, really—in return. So it is with the utmost pleasure that Gram and I offer this gift to you.

And accompanying each of the letters was a monetary gift that rendered the grandkids speechless.

As you can imagine, it was a meaningful and emotional moment for everyone. Not only did Joseph get to fulfill this wish **in his lifetime,** but he was also able to make the gifts on behalf of his late wife.

Isn't this what we all hope to create? Joseph teaches us all that we can have a life well-lived, as well as a legacy for those left behind.

Ideas to Spark, Connect & Create this week:

- Think about your own legacy. Are your intentions clear? Are they thoughtful, meaningful, and what you would want others to remember about you? Write them down here.
- Is your giving plan going to happen when you are no longer alive? Or would you like to start making meaningful gifts **within your lifetime**? What would be more meaningful to you? What would be more impactful to your recipients?

- Do you have a house of collectibles and meaningful items? Have you ever shared with others why these are so meaningful to you? What if you invited the grandkids over for a tour and some show-and-tell?
- Do you have parents, grandparents, or even an elderly neighbor who might want to give you a "tour" of all their nostalgic items throughout their house? Offer up your listening ear as they walk you down their own personal memory lane.

Notes and Thoughts

CHAPTER 38

THE DETAILS MATTER

Edward and Jane were in their seventies, recently retired and looking for a new financial advisor. They were referred to me by their best friends, who had been my clients for years. We were introduced first on the phone. Edward was very candid in explaining to me that he and Jane were interviewing several other people for this important job of managing their portfolio.

I thought our introductory conversation went great. They wanted to come to my office, however, to meet me in person before making their final decision. We set a date for the following week.

They pulled into my parking lot twenty minutes early. I could see them from my upstairs window. They drove an older model gray Mercedes. It was clear that they had gotten dressed up for our meeting. They didn't come in at first but instead sat in the front seat of the car reading the newspaper until it was time to come in.

Two minutes before the hour, they walked through the front door.

I came downstairs to greet them and offer them coffee or tea. At our office, there's always a fresh pot of coffee brewing for clients. If you like tea, we offer specialty teas from a local tea company. The tea bags are beautifully packaged. We use pottery mugs handmade by a client's daughter. From the second that a client walks into our office, we want them to feel like they are at home: comfortable and well taken care of. **I was raised to believe these types of details matter**.

I brought Edward and Jane to the second floor and welcomed them into my office. They sat on a soft loveseat, and I settled into the chair across from them. There were fresh tulips on the table between us, as well as tissues, a bowl of mints, a pad of paper, pens, and extra reading glasses close by. I trusted they felt at ease.

We began our conversation. I reiterated our process and the way we work with clients on all aspects of their financial planning. Both Edward and Jane grilled me about fees, expectations, how our relationship would go, and what would happen if they, in fact, chose to engage with my team and me. They wanted to know about my credentials and what kind of experience the members of my team had. It was a candid interview, and I felt confident their questions were thoughtfully answered.

Then Edward paused, leaned forward, and shared that he had one final question: "Is that your orange sports car parked out front?"

I hesitated for a moment.

It *was* my car. But I wasn't sure if it was going to be a selling feature in our discussion or something he'd be turned off by.

My brain was scanning for what to do or say: Do I explain to Edward that I've always loved expensive, fast, sporty cars? Do I try to justify my frivolous purchase? Would a retired couple think that my spending money on something like a sports car was a poor choice? After all, they were the opposite of flashy.

I pictured the contrast of my 500 horsepower, two-seater convertible with its metallic orange exterior parked next to their classic yet conservative Mercedes.

I took a breath. "Yes, that is my car." I braced myself for his reaction.

He replied, "Excellent! I was hoping that belonged to you. Now I know for sure that you are the right advisor for us."

He smiled warmly and reached out to shake my hand to make it official. Then he explained what he meant.

"When Jane and I passed that car walking into your office this morning, I happened to look inside. I was impressed that there was not a piece of paper nor a shred of trash, not even a drive-thru coffee cup to be found. I thought to myself, *that vehicle is meticulous, inside and out*. And I said to Jane, 'If that's hers, and that's how she treats her car—with such attention to detail—then she's probably the kind of person who would pay meticulous attention to our portfolio.'"

That was not at all what I expected him to say. I had been focusing on offering them good coffee and a comfy couch.

I had no idea that something as simple as taking care of my personal belongings would also matter.

Edward's comments reminded me that *it all matters*.

As you go about your week, keep this story in mind. When you wonder if someone is looking at you, paying attention to what you are doing (or not doing), or whether anyone cares about the small stuff—assume that they absolutely do.

Ideas to Spark, Connect & Create this week:

- What in your life needs some tidying up? Your car? Your desk drawers? Your garage? Make a plan to tackle it this week.
- What needs tidying up that only you can see: all the clutter you are storing in your brain that needs to get moved to a to-do list and organized outside of your head? A relationship that is messy and in need of an apology? An overdue thank-you? Write it down. **Then plan to handle it.**

- What obvious and not-so-obvious areas of your life are you committed to cleaning up in the next week? Take out your calendar and carve out a time to make this happen **this week**.

Notes and Thoughts

CHAPTER 39

IT MUST BE NICE

Ten years ago, a young musician named Kane Brown was the winner of his high school talent show. He impressed the audience by singing a cover of a popular song by country music star Chris Young.

What a difference a decade makes.

Ten years after his talent show debut, Kane Brown took the stage again. But this time, it was *alongside Chris Young* at the Country Music Awards. In 2021, their duet "Famous Friends" was nominated for Single of the Year, Musical Event of the Year, and Music Video of the Year. In an interview, Brown reflected on this full-circle moment and how proud he felt to have finally "made it" in country music. From his high school talent show all the way to the Country Music Awards, he had realized his dream of becoming a chart-topping star.[7]

But it took ten years to get there.

My friend Matt is selling his company at the end of the month. On the day of the closing, he will receive a large deposit of money into his checking account—a dollar amount that represents decades of risk-taking that finally paid off for him. Matt has invested his life into his business. He took chances that a non-entrepreneur would never have dared to.

In his younger years, Matt dreamed of building a wildly successful company. He wanted to earn a better-than-decent living to provide a great life for his family. He wanted to be the kind of man that his wife and baby girl would be proud of. He worked **so hard for twenty years**. Matt also took great care of his employees along the way. And like every entrepreneur, he hoped one day he would sell his company for a meaningful sum of money.

Then he found himself in the midst of a bidding war, a dream scenario: four different suitors were all trying to buy his business. That was when Matt realized he had "made it." His dream was finally coming true.

But it took twenty years to get there.

When you read about stories of success, are you immediately happy for the people? Do you get excited for their achievements? Are you impressed with their hard work and dedication?

Or do you find yourself in the more common scenario of judging them? Are you comparing yourself to them or maybe even wondering why the same success isn't happening for you?

Let's be honest.

At some point, I'll bet you've found yourself learning the news about someone's success and responding with, "It must be nice to be him."

When we make a sarcastic statement like that, we are giving zero credit to the hard work, struggles, and stress that this person had to endure to get to where they are now. Sure, it's easy to make assessments of the people who've "made it." It's easy to be judgmental, maybe even jealous. That's understandable and human to do so.

But rarely do we pause, look at the bigger picture, and give people **credit for their journey**.

I watched an interview between the singer Adele and Oprah. (BTW, you know you've "made it" when the world knows you by only your first name.) In their conversation, Adele shared candidly about her very personal struggles over the past few years and how she lost 100 pounds during that time.[8] I commented to a friend how impressed I was with Adele's recent focus on her health and well-being. My friend's immediate reaction was: *"If I had Adele's money and a personal trainer five days a week and a chef to prepare all my meals, I'd lose weight too. It must be nice to be Adele."*

My friend missed my point. She did that thing we often tend to do: judge the final outcome **but not give any credit to the journey**.

Of course, it must be comforting to be as financially secure as Adele and not have to worry about money when going through a painful divorce. Sure, there's that.

It also must be nice to be Kane Brown walking the red carpet, winning awards, and watching his songs climb to the top of the music charts. But his journey also included being homeless, living in a car, and trying to make it in the country music industry as a black artist. His experience along the way—his journey—was more than just the glitz and glam we see now.

I talked to Matt this morning on my drive to work. He will be the first to tell you that it's pretty nice to be him. **But that's because his perspective is one of complete gratitude**. Over the past week, he has had a chance to decompress and really reflect on his journey. That reflection prompted him to reach out to some people he owed a thank-you to.

He also reached out to some people to apologize.

Matt shared candidly that there were a few colleagues, vendors, and friends he was pretty demanding of during stressful moments in his career. **He reached out to all of them to humbly apologize**. He wanted them to know what an important role they played in his and his company's success and that he was sorry for ever treating them less than the awesome people they are.

Next time you see someone on television being awarded for their success or read about someone's good fortune online and think, *It must be nice to be him*, try instead to give some credit to their journey.

While you are at it, consider your own journey. Maybe **give yourself more credit**. Look at where you are and how far you have come, and recognize the incredible journey you have been on. Take a moment to remind yourself that it sure is nice to be you.

Ideas to Spark, Connect & Create this week:

- Who is someone you know, admire, and whose accomplishments impress you? What if you take a moment this week to send them an email or a personal note of acknowledgment? Tell them how much you admire their hard work. Imagine the impact that this could have on the recipient.
- Take time to reflect on your own journey. Too often, we focus on the road ahead and all the work we still must do. Rarely do we look back on the accomplishments we have already achieved, and how far along our road we have already traveled. This is a perfect moment to share the details of the journey you've been on and what you're most proud of. Tell your story to your spouse, your kids, and your grandkids . . . and be sure to give credit to those who have helped you along the way.
- Why wait? Take five minutes to jot down right here the things you are most proud of in your life so far.

Notes and Thoughts

CHAPTER 40

THE INTEGRATION SWEET SPOT

I have been preaching this, coaching this, and teaching this for decades: We all need to stop trying to find a balance between work and home. You think by mastering this so-called balance, you'll eventually find happiness.

You won't.

Think about it for a moment. If you do an outstanding job creating the perfect balance between your work life and your home life, at best, you'll be straddling 50/50 between the two.

And last I checked, a 50 percent in anything is equivalent to a letter grade of an F.

Instead, start to replace the word **balance** with **integration**.

When you integrate all aspects of *you* into everything you do, you'll discover you can have a less stressful, less chaotic, and more peaceful life.

Let me show you how.

Take this simple example. My friend Shelley is a realtor and set out to sell a record-breaking number of homes last quarter. Shelley has three children, an awesome husband, and a very demanding job. To sell that many houses meant she would have to bring clients all over town, showing multiple homes to them. She'd have to be gone on the weekends for open houses and be available at night for after-hours closing questions. It was going to take a tremendous amount of time for her to do this. But the accomplishment was something Shelley had always wanted to achieve. She would be financially rewarded for doing so. And she wanted to prove to herself she could get it done.

She called for a family meeting. During the meeting, she explained to her husband and children what this achievement would mean for her if she accomplished it. They got it because they sensed her enthusiasm. They understood that she'd be working a lot of extra hours and, for the next few weeks, might be missing some soccer games and might not be home in time for nighttime tuck-ins.

But she promised them that once the quarter was over and she achieved her goal, she'd take them all to the amusement park to celebrate—something the five of them love to do. The family started getting excited for her and for the payoff that they'd all get to participate in.

Shelley did it. She achieved the status of number one realtor in her company and made more money in one quarter than she had made in all of last year. She was elated!

In her Facebook post after reaching this career milestone, it's important to note that Shelley didn't post about herself. Instead, she shared a picture of the pep-talk letter her husband had left in her car before her last showing, telling her she was a rock star and that he believed 100 percent in her. She also shared a snip of the encouraging text message from her teenage son, listing all the rollercoasters he wanted to ride with her once she hit her goal. And last, she showed a picture of the congratulations poster created by the whole family that was hanging on the front door of her house when she got home from her last closing appointment.

This is an excellent example of integration. When you can involve your family **enthusiastically** in your work, you create a scenario where **everyone** wins when **you** win.

When you involve your family in your work goals, they get to be as excited as you. Instead of a household disappointed and resentful that you work so many hours, you get a spouse and kids who respect you and have your back.

When done thoughtfully, integration is a beautiful thing.

Integration also means finding ways to overlap your work with your hobbies.

Ken is a successful attorney who also happens to be a sommelier. This guy knows more about wine than anyone I have ever met. He can explain notes and nuances in the most interesting ways to a novice wine drinker.

His wife, Cathy, is the office manager for his law firm and also a master gardener. Their home is spectacular. It's no surprise this is where they host their annual client appreciation events: Ken and Cathy set up wine stations throughout their yard. Cathy walks the guests through her gardens, educating them along the way about each of the flowers she's grown and cultivated over the past twenty years on her property. Then the group pauses at each of Ken's wine stations. That's where Ken educates them about the types of wine they're tasting. Ken loves his work as an attorney, and he loves his successful, busy corporate clients. He also loves wine, and he loves Cathy, and Cathy loves gardening. Together they have figured out how to integrate all of these elements into a one-of-a-kind event every spring for their firms' top clients.

This is integration: taking elements of all the things you love in the separate areas of your life and bringing them together in a beautiful Venn diagram. That middle section—where all the separate circles come together—is where you want to spend most of your time.

That's the integration sweet spot.

My colleague Jason is a successful financial advisor. He also loves spending time in his woodworking shop making handcrafted wooden pens. Each pen takes about an hour from start to finish. They're time-consuming, but

Jason loves the Zen-like process of spinning the wood and carving each one personally. The pens also make great gifts.

Jason wished he could spend more time over the winter in his woodworking shop, but he was committed to taking and passing the Certified Financial Planner™ exam in March. To do this, he knew he needed to dedicate 140 hours over the winter to study.

When Jason shared with me how bummed he was about having no time for woodworking, I suggested he download as much of the audio material for the CFP exam as he could find. He listened. He brought his Bluetooth speaker into his woodshop and listened to the study material while he made his pens. Between weeknights and extra time invested on the weekends, Jason was able to clock 100 hours of studying time for the CFP exam, all the while working in his shop doing what he loves and relaxing in the process. He credits the hum of the machines and the happiness he feels in his woodworking shop to how successful he was at learning and retaining the material.

Jason passed his CFP exam on the first try, which is uncommon. He was thrilled and proud that the time he invested paid off.

And you won't be surprised that Jason also put in exactly the right amount of time to create 100 wooden pens. These are the pens he has decided to give each of his new clients this year as a very personal thank-you gift for trusting him and his team. He mailed each package with a personal message that the pen was handmade by him, specifically for them. The letter was beautifully written and shared how he made the gifted pens while also preparing for a very big exam.

This is integration.

When you really start to understand and appreciate this concept, you will no longer strive for the impossible "balance" between home and work. Instead, you will start to see how having it all—even all at once—is totally possible with deliberate planning.

When you learn how to integrate all facets of you into everything you do, **you will be happier**. When you learn how to spend more time in the middle of your Venn diagram—inside that integration sweet spot—you will feel more complete.

And when you really learn to master this, everyone in your world will start to gain a deeper appreciation for your work, your talents, and you as a complete package.

Ideas to Spark, Connect & Create this week:

- Are you torn between a hobby you wish you had more time for and the more pressing responsibilities you currently have to deal with at work and at home? Can you integrate them?
- What tedious projects need to be done at the office? Can you hire your son or daughter as

a summer intern to get them done? You'll be happy you're getting the project off your plate. Your kids will appreciate the income. That's integration.

- Write down the things you love to do, but wish you had more time for.
- Start to brainstorm how you can include others in these hobbies or projects. Where can you start to see overlap in the things you now do separately? Begin to map out the different circles of your Venn diagram, then look for ways to overlap them one at a time. Before long, you will have created your own integration sweet spot.

Notes and Thoughts

CHAPTER 41

PUTTING THE PIECES TOGETHER

Mosaics are amazing pieces of art. No two are alike. They originate from miscellaneous pieces of glass, stone, or other material of the artist's choosing. To the untrained eye, a broken piece of glass can look like scrap. It is only when the artist begins to assemble the pieces that the mosaic starts to come together.

I have seen mosaics that are uniform, with every tiny piece perfectly fit into a pattern of perfection. I've seen others that are random, abstract, and without a plan—yet the result tends to be spectacular when it's complete. Whether you're grouting stones to make a mosaic for your garden or soldering to create a stained-glass window, you have to decide where each and every piece will end up, which colors to choose, in what order, and when your piece is ultimately complete.

My friends have an art studio. I was invited last winter to join them for a day of mosaic-making. Their work is beautiful, and I was excited to try my hand at it.

To start, I had to sift through bin after bin of broken glass remnants. At first, it was hard to choose because the scraps, aside from being different colors, basically looked all the same to my untrained eye. As I started to hold each shape up to the light, I slowly began noticing that they were not alike at all. Some were transparent. Others opaque. Some had smooth edges like beach glass, while others were jagged and sharp (which also explained the first aid kit they kept nearby). I had complete freedom to choose from among the pieces, lay them out on a tray, cut and assemble them in whatever pattern I imagined, and then glue and grout them together into a permanent arrangement.

The process can take hours, sometimes days. It's like putting together a jigsaw puzzle, except that none of the pieces are precut to fit into one another. You're responsible for the spacing, cutting, sanding, and assembly. There are no instructions—just your imagination and creative freedom to put the pieces together.

I love doing this type of work. I've been back to the studio several times and have already started buying my own supplies for upcoming projects. Each mosaic I've made is different, but my friends say they have a similar style to them—like I'm developing my own art brand.

As I spend more time on my projects, I'm also learning to let go, relax, and see where each takes me. I'm getting better at it. And I've only needed two Band-Aids so far.

As I was putting the final touches on a project for my mom for Christmas, it occurred to me how mosaics are a perfect metaphor for people: We are all made up of seemingly miscellaneous parts. Some of us are colorful. Others come across as more muted. Some people are transparent, while others are quite opaque. There are people who approach life in a methodical, well-thought-out pattern. And there are others who just wing it with no clear path but can be perfectly content as the pieces of their life ultimately come together.

Like different textures and thicknesses of glass, there are certain people who come across as fragile and need to be handled with care. You know the type. Maybe this describes you. There are others who seem to be glued and soldered and grouted together with incredible strength and resilience. Maybe this describes your spouse. Or your dad.

Over time, some of us may break, and our "pieces" may need to be put back together and reinforced to be stronger. When this happens, the new mosaic may not look exactly like the old—yet there is still beauty in the broken, reassembled final product.

To me, this metaphor also helps to explain some of life's ups and downs—and how important it is to develop skill in gluing our own pieces back together when necessary.

Just as we learn to appreciate a complex piece of art, so, too, can we appreciate each of the complex people in our lives. No two of us are alike, but we can certainly learn to admire the work of art that each of us becomes.

Ideas to Spark, Connect & Create this week:

- Think about the people in your life you consider "fragile," and you perhaps tend to avoid as a result. Would it be worth taking time to reach out to one of these people this week with a new appreciation for them?
- Think about the people in your life you consider to be tough, resilient, and strong. Would it be worth taking the time to reach out to them this week with a new appreciation for the way they are?
- As you go about your week, increase your awareness of other people's art projects. Maybe it's an aunt who's knitting a sweater or a child's simple drawings. Take a moment to compliment them on their work and their attention to detail.

Notes and Thoughts

CHAPTER 42

INSPECT WHAT YOU EXPECT

"Did you brush your teeth?" I asked my son, Charlie. He was eight years old, and the expectation was that he brushed his teeth every morning before school, as well as every night before bed. I thought I was clear in my daily instruction. For whatever reason, getting him to follow through and brush his teeth was quite a challenge.

"Yup!" he would answer in the affirmative every time.

But I always had a hunch he wasn't telling the truth. So I would ask again, giving him another chance to be honest: "Are you **sure** you brushed your teeth?" And he would emphatically say yes, every time.

One night, instead of arguing back and forth and accusing him of lying, I decided to **inspect what I expect**. I walked down the hall to the bathroom and picked up Charlie's toothbrush.

Just as I thought: It was dry.

He was busted.

And from that point forward, he stepped up his game because I had stepped up mine.

Sometimes we need to inspect what we expect.

It is not enough to have an expectation for the result you are going for. It is also critical that you double-check your work, whether this pertains to your kids, your employees, or yourself.

By inspecting your work, you know for sure if it is getting done. This combination of **expectation** and **inspection**—when done consistently—often leads to success.

In the weight loss app Noom, the participants are expected to track their meals each day and eat a certain number of "green" foods (healthy, low-calorie veggies and fruits) to balance the "yellow" foods (pastas, grains, and proteins) along with the "red" foods (high-calorie foods like desserts, cheese, and alcohol). You log your meals into the app: That is the **expectation**. But you also are instructed to step on the scale every morning to weigh in—and that is the **inspection**. If you are logging the food and the scale is moving **downward**, then you've got success.

Parents, you know it is not enough to **expect** kids to do their homework. Your child will have better results when you consistently ask to **inspect** the finished product. After instituting a daily **inspection habit** over and over, your child learns that this is the drill. They miraculously begin to produce the homework—sometimes without even being asked. That is because you've set the expectation, *and* they know you'll be inspecting the results. The child now knows exactly what he or she needs to do to be successful.

This simple lesson applies to every commitment we have: *Inspect what you expect.* Imagine you have great intentions of getting up in the morning to work out. Have you set the stage for this expectation to come to fruition? Is your alarm set early enough? Are your workout clothes and sneakers laid out the night before waiting for you? Do you have a plan to meet someone at the gym for accountability—your friend or your personal trainer? Have you preselected the online class you and your BFF are going to take together? This is the inspection part of the commitment.

Without it, all you have is wishful thinking.

Inspect what you expect. My mentor, Paul, taught me this lesson twenty-five years ago. Who knew how many times and in how many areas this would be so incredibly useful in my life? I hope you find that this simple extra step of accountability will make a difference in your life as well.

Ideas to Spark, Connect & Create this week:

- Think about an area in your life where you have difficulty following through. Ask yourself (even better, write it down): What's the **expectation** I have for this goal?

- Then look at your **inspection process**: Is there something you could implement that would ensure your success? Maybe you would be willing to try one of the following:
  - Download an app to track your goal.
  - Create a page in your journal to track the goal. Before long, you will see you've got a habit.
  - Find an accountability partner to check in with.
  - Find an accountability partner to do the activity with.
  - Set an alarm on your watch, your Alexa, or your Google device to remind you every single day to get in action.
  - Plan a reward for yourself when you hit a streak goal (twenty days in a row of meditation or ten weeks in a row of working out consistently). A reward can definitely increase your motivation.

Notes and Thoughts

CHAPTER 43

FEEDBACK IS A GIFT

"Feedback is a gift." That's what I was told in my first meeting with my coach many years ago.

And to put this lesson into practice, he explained, we need to not only **give** feedback but also **receive** it with gratitude.

Easier said than done.

As a financial advisor, I am in the *giving feedback* business. When I tell clients they need to save more money for retirement, I am giving them candid feedback that what they have done up to this point in planning for their future is not adequate. This is not easy.

Some people receive feedback well. I like to refer to this type of person as *coachable*. Others resist, get defensive, and ultimately don't implement the advice they've been given. In my business, people who resist feedback are more challenging to work with. It's hard to create any positive impact or change with clients who aren't willing to listen to feedback, take it in, and take some action.

How often do you work on your "giving and receiving feedback" skills? For me, I've been working on this for decades. It takes practice.

I was thinking about some feedback I gave to a coaching client last week. She belongs to a cohort of financial advisors I work with monthly. She was complaining that she was disappointed in our group and that she wasn't getting much value from our work together.

Before reacting, I asked if she had participated in all our monthly calls. She shared that she had only been able to make it to one of the last five classes I had taught.

I next asked if she had been completing our weekly homework assignments. She hadn't. She confessed that between all the activities and stress she had been dealing with at work and at home, she'd been too busy to complete the homework.

I asked her how the tracking of her quarterly goals was coming along. She candidly shared that she hadn't tracked anything in eight weeks and had somewhere lost her momentum.

Last, I asked her how she felt about all the great ideas that were being shared in the private Facebook group. She said she "doesn't do Facebook."

Clearly, I could see an opportunity to provide feedback.

"Julie, would you like some feedback?"

This is an important step: Ask permission first before giving someone feedback. I don't know too many people who appreciate unsolicited advice.

Julie said she was open to hearing my thoughts.

I commented, "I can completely understand why you're disappointed in the group. I think you'd find it much more valuable if you committed to following the steps in our program, completing the homework assignments, and tracking progress toward your goals. The assignments are designed to be progressive, and the momentum builds throughout the course of the year. But if you're not doing most of the work, I think disappointment is going to be the only reasonable outcome."

I paused. That was the feedback.

But then I asked a follow-up question. After providing feedback, I find that it's helpful to also ask some thoughtful questions.

"Is there some area in your life where you are finding real satisfaction and accomplishment these days?"

Julie answered without hesitation, "Oh, yes! Definitely in my health and fitness. I dropped twelve pounds since January, and I've kept them off. I'm stronger and more flexible than I've been in years."

"And why do you think this is working so well for you?"

She answered enthusiastically, "It's because I show up for my appointments with my trainer three times a week. I'm totally present during my workouts, and I do every single assigned cardio and strength workout he gives me. On the days when I'm not with him, I report back to him what I've done for my self-guided workouts. Having that one-on-one accountability works great for me."

"That makes total sense. Would you be willing to apply that same principle to our coaching group to see if you get better results?"

Julie's brow furrowed. "What do you mean?"

"Here's my advice: Pick someone within the group to be your accountability partner—someone you respect, maybe even someone who intimidates you a little bit. Just like you show up for your personal trainer, I want you to commit to showing up for your accountability partner for the next quarter and see what happens."

Not surprisingly, she loved the idea. In fact, she became re-engaged immediately. She also knew exactly the person she wanted to partner with.

What started out as a complaint from Julie turned into a thank-you at the end of our conversation. She agreed to take on the assignment and get back to me at the end of the next quarter with her feedback.

Feedback, when accompanied by an idea or a proposed solution, can be well-received. Instead of telling Julie she's a mediocre member of our group for not doing the work, I had to accompany my feedback with an idea that would resonate with her.

Feedback is a gift.

When we give it in a caring and genuine way and offer a solution, people are grateful.

When was the last time you *received* feedback? Did you take it on with gratitude?

If I look back over the past few months at the feedback I received graciously versus the feedback I interpreted as criticism (and where I got immediately defensive), I can see in hindsight that there was a clear distinction between how the feedback was delivered in each instance.

Feedback accompanied by an idea for how to do things better feels useful. Feedback that's just critical with no ideas or alternatives feels judgemental and upsetting.

Feedback **can be** a gift. We just have to remember to deliver it with compassion and to receive it with open-mindedness and appreciation.

Ideas to Spark, Connect & Create this week:

- Is there someone you need to provide feedback to? Even if it has been a long time in coming, consider that holding back and not offering feedback is doing them a disservice.
- Who is the person you need or want to reach out to?
- Before you offer this person feedback, take a few minutes to prepare for the conversation. How

will you deliver your message with kindness and compassion? Are you prepared with some ideas or possible solutions?

- If someone offers you feedback this week—solicited or unsolicited—and it feels initially like criticism, pause for a moment. Before getting offended or defensive, ask the person for suggestions on how you could do things differently the next time. This takes practice, but it is a humbling and helpful skill for us all to develop.

Notes and Thoughts

CHAPTER 44
BUS STOPS & DROP-OFFS

While driving to the office the other day, I couldn't help but notice the number of school buses on the road. That's when I remembered that it was the first day of school for all the children in our town.

I ended up driving directly behind one of the shiny yellow buses. Every hundred yards or so, the bus driver would slow down, flash his warning lights, and stop to pick up more kids standing on the street corner.

Waiting on the sidewalk up ahead was a small group of children in their plaid uniforms—a style that hasn't changed much since my Catholic school days. I noticed a young girl next to her mom. She was wearing a perfectly pressed uniform, a backpack practically the size of her body, and rainbow glitter sneakers. She was adorable except for one thing: She was crying uncontrollably.

As the bus put its blinker on and pulled over to the right, the young girl turned to her mom, threw her arms around her, and sobbed.

I watched from my car as the moment unfolded. I knew the feeling, having been through it *many* years ago with my own son.

I also knew that the mother had only a few seconds to make a big parenting decision: *Does she put her crying child on the bus or not?*

As the other kids were excitedly moving up the bus stairs, I watched as the mom bent down and got face-to-face with the little girl. She gave her a huge hug, lovingly spun her little body around, and nudged her toward the bus.

The little girl wiped her tears, climbed the stairs with tears still in her eyes, and disappeared from my view.

I watched as Mom continued to wave enthusiastically and kept giving her daughter the two-thumbs-up signal. She stood there until the bus drove away, gave one last big wave, turned around, and let herself burst into tears.

Letting go is so hard.

As parents, we know it's the right thing to do. But letting go is never easy. We must trust that we've done years' worth of work to prepare our children for these big life transitions. We give them a hug and attempt to send them confidently on their way—even if it sometimes means they are accompanied by tears.

We all hope to have kids who are well-adjusted and who will happily hop on the bus on that first day of school.

But sometimes, that's not what we get.

Those of you who've recently gone through this type of transition know exactly what I mean. September is the time of year when many of us have to practice letting go.

I've been following dozens of friends on social media who have been posting pictures of their children's newly decorated dorm rooms. Was this you? Did you just drop your "baby" off at college? Did you predict how you wanted the experience to go? You imagined that you would drive onto campus, enthusiastically carry your son or daughter's boxes up the stairs, set up their new bedding, get their stuff organized, give them some final words of wisdom, and say a not-too-tearful goodbye, right?

But when the moment comes, sometimes it doesn't go quite as planned.

I'll never forget moving my son, Charlie, into his dorm his freshman year. We arrived shortly after his roommate, Evan, did. Between the two boys, there was so much stuff in that tiny space I didn't know how it was all going to come together. I started unpacking the box of bedding and pillows. Evan's mom was trying to get her son's suitcases unpacked but was struggling to fit all his belongings into the small college-issued dresser. She asked Evan if it was okay if she consolidated all his socks and underwear into one drawer. I could see she was getting emotional, trying to make it all work. And I could also see her son was getting embarrassed by his mother's questions.

"Hey, Evan," I asked, "would you mind going out to our car with Charlie to grab his last two boxes?" The boys exited the room. Evan's mom looked at me and started to cry.

I tried to assure her by reminding her (and me), "It's going to be okay." We proceeded to have a special mom moment, talking about how strange it was to be dropping our boys off at school. We agreed we just had to believe that they would adjust in the coming days and weeks.

A couple of minutes later, the boys reappeared with the last of Charlie's things. All that was left was to make the beds. I started putting pillowcases on the pillows. That's when Evan stated, "Okay, Mom. I'm good. You can go."

Evan's mom stood still, holding a flat sheet. He walked forward, gently took the sheet from her hands, and asked her to leave. No final emotional hug, no emotional goodbye. She waved and slowly walked away.

At that moment, I understood what Evan needed.

And my heart also broke for his mom.

I helped the boys get their beds made, and then it was clear that Charlie was ready for me to leave as well. He said he'd walk me to the car.

First, I took a few final pictures of the dorm room. Their stuff was mostly organized. Charlie packed far too many pairs of sneakers but refused to let me take any home. At least I could exit knowing there were clean sheets and comforters on both boys' beds.

Before I left the room, I asked Evan for his mom's cell phone—just in case we ever needed to communicate with each other. He gave it to me.

As Charlie and I walked toward my car, he asked me to please not cry. I promised him I wouldn't, at least until he was out of sight. He was excited to be there. We hugged. I got into my car. He waved as he walked back toward his dorm. And surprisingly, I held it together.

But I did take a minute to text Evan's mother a picture of her son's room, as well as a picture of the two boys on their first day of college. She thanked me, told me how much she appreciated my message, and said that the photos were just what she needed to know her son would be okay. I drove away from campus feeling brave and proud.

I continued feeling this way until I got home. I walked into my house, put my purse on the counter, and opened the fridge for a cold drink. That's when I saw a container of leftover buffalo chicken wings—Charlie's dinner from the night before—and realized that he would not be back anytime soon to eat his leftovers.

I burst into tears, nostalgically hugging the Styrofoam container of cold chicken wings.

Whether you are dropping off your kindergartener on his first day of school or dropping off your college student for his first semester away from home, it's never easy letting them go. You could be putting your daughter on a plane for a year of studying abroad or walking her down the aisle on her wedding day. No matter the circumstances, I'm not sure we are ever totally prepared for these gigantic moments of change and transition. And they all require some letting go.

So do just that.

Have faith that each of these milestones helps us all to become more confident and braver. After the tears dry, we must trust that we—and they—will be just fine.

Ideas to Spark, Connect & Create this week:

- Do you have a big transition coming up? If so, it might be helpful to have your sappy moments and tearful goodbyes in advance of the actual day. Maybe plan a family dinner the night before. Take that time to share with your child how much you love them, how proud you are of their upcoming transition, and that you know they're going to do great. This simple conversation might save you from having to give a tearful speech the following day. Your child might also appreciate this proactive gesture.

- Know someone who is dropping a child off at college, taking their little one to kindergarten or preschool for the first time, or maybe even becoming empty-nesters this fall? Reach out to them. A thoughtful text, phone call, or card in the mail acknowledging this bittersweet moment could make all the difference for someone you care about. A little empathy goes a long way during these emotional moments.

Notes and Thoughts

CHAPTER 45

THE BEST MONEY YOU'LL EVER SPEND

When I met up with my friend Jillian recently, she arrived looking exhausted. Before I could say anything, she commented on herself, "I know, I know. I look terrible. I had the worst night's sleep. My mattress is so uncomfortable."

I asked the obvious question, "Why don't you get a new mattress?"

She went on to say that her husband sleeps poorly, too, and that their mattress is lumpy and squeaky. It is the same one they got when they were married, which makes the mattress officially twenty years old. They had been intending to get a new bed for years but hadn't taken the time to go to the mattress store to choose something new.

I shared with Jillian that when we had purchased a new mattress several years ago, it made a gigantic difference in our quality of sleep (and, ultimately, our quality of life). I told her empathetically I never knew how uncomfortable our old bed had been until we finally got the new one.

Jillian acknowledged how ridiculous the situation had become. She said she didn't know how silly her excuses sounded until she explained them out loud to me. In that moment, she committed to making a date with her husband to shop for a new mattress.

Two weeks later, Jillian called to say she felt like a renewed person. "This new bed is like sleeping on a cloud. Seriously, this is the best sleep we have had in years. And this was the best money we've spent in a long time."

Another friend recently had Lasik eye surgery to correct her vision. She had been wearing glasses since second grade. She is now fifty-two. A few weeks after the surgery, she shared with me that she feels like she is experiencing a different quality of life. To wake up in the middle of the night and be able to see the alarm clock perfectly or to go swimming in the lake and open her eyes underwater—it's nothing short of a miracle to her! She said, "I don't know why I waited until now to do this. It's the best $3,000 I have ever spent."

Take a moment to think about something in your life that is an inconvenience. What is it that you continue to tolerate, even though you know you could fix it or improve it?

I posed this question to a group of friends: Tell me about something you "invested" in, even though it felt expensive or luxurious at the time, yet turned out to be the best money you've ever spent.

Here are some of the things they shared:

A gas stove: *When I bought my house, it came with an electric stove. I hated it, yet I used it for five years because there was nothing technically wrong with it. I love to cook, and an electric stove is not ideal. When I finally committed and bought my new six-burner gas stove, it was the best purchase I had ever made. Worth every cent! And I gave my electric stove to my daughter for her new apartment—which she was thrilled about.*

A personal trainer: *I hated going to the gym because it was overwhelming. I'd only use the machines that were familiar to me and ended up doing the same routine every time. I did this for years. When I finally hired a personal trainer this past summer, it changed everything. I'm stronger, leaner, healthier—and I'm more committed to my workouts because my trainer is at the gym waiting enthusiastically for me three times a week. Sure, it's expensive, **but compared to what**? I finally decided my health was worth the money. Who knew it would also turn out to be an investment in my happiness!*

A new car: *For years, I prided myself on driving my old Honda Accord with 200,000 miles on it. I had no car payment, and I wanted to keep it that way for as long as possible. But in the past year, every time I drove the old clunker, I worried it would break down. I realized the car kept me from going very far because I feared it wasn't reliable. I finally decided to lease a new Accord. I had no idea how awesome the upgraded technology would be, how much better on gas it would be, and how enjoyable it would be to take road trips again. It even has built-in navigation! My new car is a game-changer, and I feel more confident knowing it's reliable. It might sound weird, but even the lease payment makes me happy. I'm spending money on something I enjoy every day.*

We all have inconveniences we tolerate, even though we know we can fix or eliminate them. What comes to mind for you? **Do not overthink it**. Instead, consider that investing money in that item or that experience could improve your quality of life. Who knows, maybe your decision to make a proactive change will inspire those around you to do the same.

Ideas to Spark, Connect & Create this week:

- What's the best money *you've* ever spent? Was it on a vacation? Did you splurge on an experience that still feels vivid and memorable? Was it something decadent, and you have no regrets *even to this day* because it was worth every penny? Write it down right now to remind yourself of those feelings of happiness and satisfaction.

- What's the thing in your life that you are still tolerating but now might be ready to upgrade, change, fix, or eliminate altogether?

- Think of your loved ones. Is there something your elderly father or aunt is tolerating because the thought of changing it is overwhelming to them? Maybe Dad needs new hearing aids, or your aunt needs to start cleaning out the clutter in her home. Could you help them take the next small step toward making this change?

Notes and Thoughts

CHAPTER 46

GIVE THEM HOPE

When I was a brand-new financial advisor, I got paid twice a month with a paper check. I would go to my office mailbox, and there would either be an envelope with a clear window on the front, an indication that there was a check inside, or there would be a plain envelope, which meant no check—just a statement explaining why my income was zero for that pay period. Such was the risk I took when I chose to become a 100 percent commission advisor.

Our office mailboxes were lined up against a wall. Advisors would wait for the mail clerk to put our envelopes in our respective cubbies. On one of those paydays, I was standing next to a colleague, Greg, who had been in the business for ten years. I was only in my second year. He was dressed in a beautiful suit, cufflinks, and Ferragamo shoes. I was not. I was wearing a nice outfit that had been charged to my Ann Taylor credit card and had not yet been paid for.

I noticed my colleague's envelope had a clear window. Mine did not.

I had optimistically hoped that a few of my cases would have closed in time, but they hadn't. I was working hard, borrowing money to pay my expenses, and barely breaking even. My efforts did not yet match my revenue in those early years.

Greg opened his envelope, turned to me, and sarcastically stated, "Someday, you might get one of these!" He brazenly showed me his check. It was for $67,000.

Sixty-seven thousand dollars.

In a matter of seconds, my thoughts went something like this:

- Holy *&$# That is so much money!
- Why does he get that much while I get nothing?
- I am so much smarter than him.
- This doesn't seem fair.
- This business is hard.
- I am so bummed right now.
- This sucks.
- I want what he has.
- How long will it take to get paid that much?
- I must keep working. I need more time.
- Eventually, it **WILL** come together, won't it?

- Why would he show me that check? That was obnoxious.
- I'm kind of glad he showed me that check. It means it's possible for me.

That moment in my career could have gone either way: I could quit, or I could choose to keep going.

I chose the latter, thank goodness. But that's because I had other people—not like Greg—who were encouraging me and giving me hope along the way.

There was a ton of struggle in the beginning. My colleagues seemed successful and confident, and I was neither. I had to keep reminding myself about my long-term vision. I knew I wanted a future where I would be financially stable and have consistent cash flow. I wanted to one day buy nice clothes that I didn't have to charge on my credit card. I wanted to be a provider for my family, fund my future children's college accounts, and ultimately save for retirement.

In hindsight, I now understand I was not alone in my thinking. Many young people who are new in their careers—regardless of their industry or specialty—feel the same way early on: defeated, frustrated, and sometimes understandably jealous of others' success.

If you are someone who has "made it," and you have time and wisdom on your side, please encourage young people to keep the faith. Ask how they are doing. Tell them what it was like when you were them and share humbly and confidently about where you are now.

We have to remind them how important it is to believe in themselves and **keep on going**. Even when it's exhausting. We must remind them that we believe in them. And when they are ready to quit because they've lost confidence and haven't given their careers enough time, we have to remind them, "Hang in there, kiddo."

If you are new in your business and struggling, I'm here to tell you: Hang in there, kiddo. It takes a **long time** to make it, to feel confident, and not second-guess your career choice.

I believe it is our responsibility to give them hope.

I know you are busy. I am too.

But taking a moment out of your day to reach out to a young worker to give them encouragement will matter. Commit to inviting a young person out for lunch at a nice restaurant and offer to give them an hour of your time, just because.

Maybe you think you're too far along in your career, and you won't be able to relate to a younger person. You might find yourself questioning whether your perspective is still relevant to a person brand-new in his or her career.

I bet you $67,000 that it will be.

Ideas to Spark, Connect & Create this week:

- For younger people: Find yourself a role model or mentor in your field. What is it about them that you admire? Invite them for a coffee and share your admiration for them and your perspective thus far about your own work experience. Ask if they have any career or life advice for you. Then be sure to listen.

- For those of you who are more experienced: Find yourself a mentee or protégé. Invest time in the next generation. Share your insights, words of wisdom, and perspective with them. Encourage them. Give them hope for their own future. And let them know you will be there for them if they need you.

Notes and Thoughts

CHAPTER 47

THE BEST & WORST PURCHASE

Mid-pandemic, I went online and ordered a Peloton bike. Kim and I had made a commitment to staying healthy, eating well, and working out on a regular basis. It seemed the perfect time to set these goals—we had nowhere to go, our kids were out of the house, and we had nothing to do but stay home indefinitely.

Like most exercise equipment during that time, my bike was back-ordered. It took eight weeks to get it delivered. When it arrived on a Friday afternoon, I was so excited to test it out.

Initially, I wasn't sure how to clip the shoes in. The seat was too low, the handlebars too high. Eventually, I was able to make all the necessary tweaks and adjustments for the bike to fit me just right.

I am proud to say that I have been using my bike every single week for two years. I love it. I know exactly what to expect when I get on it. I appreciate the instructors' ideas and encouragement. I'm motivated by the community of friends and strangers I ride with. There is so much variety in terms of music choices—no matter my mood, I can find the right tunes. Last week I rode to Fleetwood Mac, as well as to songs from Broadway. Within the Peloton app, I'm easily able to track my progress. I appreciate that I can push hard for a twenty-minute morning ride with an instructor, or I can choose a leisurely scenic option while I listen to a podcast.

The Peloton bike was a purchase I made after giving it much thought, doing research, and weighing my options. I talked with a lot of people about their Peloton experience to gather helpful endorsements. I have no regrets about buying it. In fact, I feel like I have already gotten my money's worth in just these two years.

Have you ever made a significant purchase and were so happy about your choice to do so? That's how I feel about my bike.

The Peloton bike is one of the best purchases I have ever made.

A year later, I also decided to buy Peloton stock. After all, I knew I wasn't the only person enamored with my bike. Many people—millions, in fact—had made the same purchase as me during the pandemic. No surprise that the company did incredibly well during 2020 and 2021.

On the day I bought Peloton stock, I thought I was quite savvy. Although the market had been going up, Peloton stock had experienced a slight dip in price. I assumed it was from the recall they had with their new treadmill. But that was just a hunch. I did no research. I did not consider that gyms were reopening and people would begin canceling their Peloton subscriptions. I didn't look into who was running their company, what their overhead was, or that they were paying a significant premium to fly bikes from overseas via airplanes because cargo ships were taking too long. I didn't look at the historical price of the stock nor what any outside source was predicting for the company moving forward. Unlike my very deliberate purchase of the bike, my Peloton stock purchase was reactionary, on a whim, and not well-thought-out.

At all.

I bought the stock for $128 a share. I didn't look to see that the fifty-two-week high had been $129. I made my purchase as the stock began its downward slide.

Today, as I write this story, Peloton stock is selling for $9 a share. **I am officially down 93 percent**.

Peloton stock is one of the worst purchases I have ever made.

Today—I kid you not—my bike is worth more in value than my stock.

Have you ever made a purchase and soon after regretted it? Maybe it was an expensive watch, an overpriced pair of sneakers, or a pricey vacation—and afterward, you wished you could go back and undo it.

Me too.

I'm not saying that the Peloton stock will never recover. I'm simply pointing out that I didn't follow my own advice: Instead of sticking to tried-and-true principles and making a stock purchase based on sound fundamentals, I was driven by emotion and spontaneity. This is not the advice I would have given to a client, yet I took it for myself.

I find it (almost) funny that the decision to purchase a Peloton bike was a deliberate investment in my health and wellness. At the same time, the purchase of the Peloton stock was mathematically one of the worst things I have ever placed in my portfolio.

My timing for one purchase was excellent. My timing for the other was terrible.

As I rode my bike this morning, I found myself feeling grateful for how well it has served me these past two years and how strong my legs have gotten. I appreciate the sweat and stress I am able to leave on the bike following every ride. No buyer's remorse here.

As I think about my plummeting Peloton stock, understandably, I wish I'd never made that purchase.

There comes a time, however, when we have to move on.

At some point, regret and disappointment no longer serve us. We have to forgive ourselves—and trust that there was a lesson to be learned from our mistakes, big or small.

That's what I've chosen to do with my stock: forgive myself and move on.

Keep my story in mind as you enjoy the year, go on a much-deserved vacation with your family, and maybe even treat yourself to some new things for the holidays. We all work hard for the money we earn. Let us invest time and effort into thinking in advance about purchases we are considering making, assess their potential impact on us, and proceed after thoughtful consideration.

Ideas to Spark, Connect & Create this week:

- Is there a big-ticket item you are considering purchasing? What research do you need to do first before committing to buying it? Do you feel like you have enough information to decide with confidence and not second-guess yourself after the fact?
- Is there something you have purchased in the past and wish you had not? Can you finally forgive yourself for doing so?
- If the item you regret buying still bothers you, can you return it? Even if it's past the return deadline, sometimes you can politely explain your story and hope that customer service will empathize and allow the return to happen.
- Can you repurpose the item (give it to a friend, regift it, donate it) to someone who will love it and appreciate it more than you? Putting it in the hands of someone who will appreciate it might make all the difference in your ability to move on from it.

Notes and Thoughts

CHAPTER 48

GREEN AND GROWING

Today, for me, marks the end of the fall season. Leaves have changed colors and are now falling off the trees. The squirrels have worked overtime getting prepped for the winter. Birds have already flown south for warmer weather. And all the hydrangea bushes throughout our landscaping have shut down—just another reminder that the year is almost over.

I pulled into my parking spot this morning, however, and noticed the small rose bush still filled with beautiful roses, despite the chilly evening weather threatening its viability. Its heartiness and bright orange color—growing toward the November sunshine—were noteworthy. I thought, *What lesson am I supposed to take from this interesting juxtaposition in our landscaping*?

To me, I saw the two plants as symbols of the way many people define this time of the year. Some will identify with the hydrangeas with an attitude that says,

"It's over, it's too late to try anything new, and it's time to move on and start again next year."

Yet that rose bush, still thriving and blossoming, might be the thing you identify with. While others have understandably called it quits for this year, maybe you're the person who believes you still have growth left in you. Maybe you're the one pushing to reach your year-end goals. You're the one still innovating in your business when others are looking forward to time off. You're the schoolteacher still keeping your students engaged despite all the holiday excitement and distraction ahead of them.

While others are packing up and shutting down their year, you're that lush rose bush, green and growing, despite your surroundings.

If this describes you, congratulations! Continue to make the most of your calendar year and squeeze as much as you can out of each remaining day. The seeds you are planting now will show up in a future, fruitful harvest. Your hard work and perseverance will eventually be worth it.

If you're the hydrangea, stop and ask yourself: What would it take to breathe some new life into me during these last few weeks of the year? What help do I need to have a positive, accomplishing, something-to-be-proud-of last quarter? Who is the person who can help me get there? My team? My spouse? A great friend who might be willing to join me for some year-end accountability?

A wise friend once told me, "In life, you are either green and growing or ripe and rotting. One is vibrant and lush and beautiful. The other is brown and smelly and shriveling up. These are your two options. But the good news is that you get to choose which one you want to be."

Choose wisely.

Ideas to Spark, Connect & Create this week:

- Where are you green and growing in your life? In what areas are you lush and vibrant and full of life? Write them down.
- Where can you take some of that energy and expand it?
- Is there any area in your life where you feel like you are ripe and rotting? What needs to be done to turn that around? How can you bring a more green-and-growing approach to that aspect of life?

Notes and Thoughts

CHAPTER 49

DEATH GRIP

Last winter, my partner, Kim, and I went cross-country skiing in New Hampshire. We were seeking fresh snow, groomed trails, and a "real" place to use our new skis (rather than our backyard). All roads led us to Gunstock Mountain.

As we pulled into the parking lot, we were surprised to see dozens and dozens of very tall and fit teenagers unloading from school buses. As the students gathered with their groups and started putting their numbered bibs on, it became clear they were gearing up to compete against the other high school cross-country ski teams also arriving.

For a few minutes, this seemed irrelevant to us. We parked the car, grabbed our gear, and walked up the hill to put our skis on. As we approached a trail marked green (i.e., easy), we were informed that the high school students would be using that section for the rest of the day for their event. We, however, were welcome to ski on any blue (hard) or black diamond (very hard) trails.

If you're a good skier, this probably would have seemed like no big deal.

We are novices. In fact, until we bought our skis last winter, neither of us had been cross-country skiing, ironically, since high school.

Kim and I proceeded with caution as we made our way to the blue trails.

The trail began with a seemingly subtle downhill slope. We were off!

I held onto my poles as I began to pick up speed. I then tried to swish smoothly from side-to-side as if I were on downhill skis. I had forgotten that cross-country skis don't work that way. Only your toes are clipped in, not the whole boot. Your boots are soft and have no hard plastic support, your heels are loose, and there is no way to easily "swoosh" side-to-side gracefully. At all.

In one slow, awkward movement, I wiped out. It took me a moment to remember how to lean on my side and position my body to get back up. I reassembled, gripped my poles, pulled myself to a standing position, and we were off again.

But I was clearly out of my comfort zone.

At the end of the first gradual decline was a sharp right turn. I slowed down enough to make the safe transition. In front of us was a beautiful trail that stretched deeper into the woods, snowy and quiet and flat for about 100 feet. At that moment, I was relieved and thought, *This is what I remember cross-country skiing to be like: beautiful, tranquil, flat, and straight.*

After this nice stretch, the trail ended with a steep uphill climb.

Yes, a climb.

I took a deep breath, pointed my toes outward and positioned my skis into a V-shape to ascend it. I also clenched my poles with a death grip: Every move upward needed to be accompanied by a simultaneous jabbing of poles into the snowy/rocky/icy hill to make any progress. For every step forward, I slid on the ice a bit backward. It took fifteen minutes to get to the top of the hill, where there was a plateau. I caught my breath and reassessed the situation.

At the top of the hill, I found myself at a crossroads. We could go left and climb another steeper hill, or we could go right and begin the descent.

I turned around to see what Kim was thinking. That's when I saw that she had unclipped from her skis somewhere in the middle of that icy hill, carried her equipment to the top, and was in the process of putting her skis back on. As she tried balancing to get her toe into the ski's clip, she completely tipped over. I attempted to ski toward her to grab her pole, but instead, I skied right over it. Now she was on the ground, I was heading toward the ground, and my skis were completely on top of her poles.

To add to this unathletic scene, imagine that a few days earlier, I had gone to the salon to have my hair colored a deep magenta. I thought it would be a "fun" winter color. With the skiing and climbing and my significantly elevated heart rate, however, I had begun sweating. The heat and the moisture inside my ski hat produced something you've probably never seen before: Picture light magenta patches of color seeping through a beige wool hat. This was funny to me many days later. But not at all in that moment.

After Kim was able to extricate her poles from beneath my skis, we opted to cautiously coast downhill rather than keep the uphill climb going. We agreed this would likely bring our adventure to a close sooner than later.

I went first.

The downhill cruise was lovely and gradual and pretty straightforward. Then up ahead, I could see a final left turn we'd somehow have to maneuver. I gripped my poles so tightly on the curve that I snapped the top piece off my right pole, and the strap broke. I had to stuff the strap into my pocket when I realized reassembly didn't seem likely until we got to the car. We continued.

My anxiety decreased only when I could finally see the lodge up ahead. Next to it, the high school kids were cheering wildly for their friends as they finished the final lap of their race. I, too, was cheering—quietly in my head—that Kim and I had made it back to flat land and a vision of our car in the not-so-far distance.

As I waited a few moments for Kim to finish her descent, I found myself reflecting on the past hour, wishing I had better skills, wishing I was more confident in my skiing ability, and wishing that I could have made the turns without falling down. That's precisely when Kim skied up alongside me, carefully raised her hand, and high-fived me. I looked at her with confusion. She enthusiastically pointed out what a success our day was: We had burned a lot of calories. We had used our new skis as planned. And, thank goodness, we had broken no bones. As if that weren't enough, she stated, we should be proud we navigated a blue trail across unexpectedly challenging terrain despite our rusty skills.

And you know, she was absolutely right.

Life often presents us with challenges and discomfort. We also have choices along the way: uphill or downhill? Climb with skis on, or unclip, carry your equipment, and be safer? Getting the job done doesn't always mean looking good in the process. Sometimes accomplishment is hard to see when it's hidden between anxiety and magenta sweat.

No matter how awkward our climb or descent, we should always take time to appreciate our hard work. And sometimes, we have to get through a death grip experience before we earn the high-five at the end.

Ideas to Spark, Connect & Create this week:

- What experience have you had recently that you deemed a failure? Why? How did you define *failure* in that moment?
- Is there a way to retell that failure story but with a different ending? Can you find a different—more positive—lesson within it?
- Is there something you've been avoiding doing because you worry you won't be very good at it? Like learning to play the guitar, going skiing for the first time in twenty years, or quitting your job to be a freelancer like you've always dreamed of doing? What would happen if you did that, and it was a total success? Write down what that would feel like.
- Now's your chance to commit to trying something new, something seemingly scary, and take it on despite your feelings.

Notes and Thoughts

CHAPTER 50

A PIZZA & A TIP

I went to pick up a pizza for dinner on my drive home. It was a cold night, and snowflakes were starting to stick as they landed on my Jeep's windshield. I had the Christmas music cranked up and was feeling festive.

Plus, I love pizza.

I walked into the restaurant and approached the pickup counter. The woman working there was clearly not feeling the same holiday vibe as me. She flatly asked what my name was. I told her.

Without looking up, she said, "That'll be $24.50."

I took out thirty dollars from my wallet. She handed the change back to me without comment or eye contact. I could see that my pizza was just coming out of the oven.

As I waited for the pizza maker to box it up, I noticed a bowl on the counter: **Tips Appreciated**.

And the bowl—no surprise—was empty.

I had two conflicting thoughts:

1. The woman at the pickup counter is a bit grouchy, so it makes sense that the tip bowl is empty, but...
2. Maybe she's having a bad day. Maybe she hates her job. Maybe this is not "the most wonderful time of the year" for her, for whatever reason.

I took the five-dollar bill and the coins she had just handed me and dropped them into her tip bowl.

A moment later, she came around the corner and plopped my pizza box on the counter. In that same instant, she spotted the five-dollar bill and change in her once-empty bowl.

She smiled wide. Her eyes became instantly friendly. She made direct eye contact and said, "Thanks so much, honey! You have yourself a great night! Enjoy your pizza! I *really* appreciate this."

In an instant, her entire demeanor shifted.

Could my small five-dollar gesture have turned her night around? Maybe.

I walked back to my car and continued thinking about her on my drive home. How often do we have an opportunity to positively impact someone with a simple act of kindness or generosity? Isn't that what the holiday spirit is all about?

This is a great time of the year to think about your **tipping philosophy**. Are you a generous tipper? Do you leave 20 percent no matter the service? Do you tip solely on performance?

What is your philosophy about this?

People who work in the service industry and rely on tips have a lot of unpredictability in their jobs. They can give a customer their best effort, but that doesn't necessarily mean the customer is going to leave a tip commensurate with the server's hard work or attentiveness. A waitress can be excellent, but if the food coming out of the kitchen is subpar, a customer might choose to leave a small (or no) tip as a result.

That's a bummer.

What if we all shifted our thinking and upgraded our "tipping philosophy"?

I challenge you to push yourself beyond your normal tip-giving over the next month and see what opportunities come up to make a bigger difference:

- Think about your babysitter and the impact she has on your children all year—what if you Venmoed her a little bit extra this week as a sign of your appreciation, just because?
- What about those teenagers bagging your groceries every week? Sure, you get frustrated when they put canned goods on top of your loaf of bread. Remember, they're teenagers with

jobs, which is not common and quite notable. Could you slip them a few bucks and wish them a great weekend?

- My friend leaves a basket on her front porch all December with snacks, chips, and candy canes. The sign says: "Thank you, Amazon, FedEx, UPS, and USPS, for getting my packages here! Help yourself to a snack!"

- Think about the guy who plows your driveway super-early after a snowstorm so you can get to work on time—what if you paid his invoice, added a little extra, and wrote THANK YOU across the invoice? Better yet, what if you carefully shuffled out to your driveway when he arrived and handed him a hot cup of coffee to enjoy while he plowed? How great would that be?

- My friend owns a company, and all his employees have a company credit card. His rule is that if you are ever using the company card in a restaurant, you must always leave a 20 percent tip. He wants them to practice being generous—even if he's the one ultimately paying the bill.

- My mom is notorious for stopping at Dunkin Donuts and getting a cold drink for police officers working road details on a hot day or a hot chocolate for them in the winter. Small gestures = gigantic impact.

o   A friend of mine has several gallon-size resealable bags in her car. Each is filled with a pair of lightly used gloves, a warm pair of socks, a few snacks, and a bottle of water. She hands them out to homeless people she sees on her commute to work. She does this all winter. Her kind gesture literally warms people up.

What is *your* kind gesture going to be? What change could you make in your routine that could put a smile on someone's face?

Even better, involve your kids or grandkids. Explain to them what it means to tip generously, how to show gratitude, and when to spread extra holiday cheer. Lead by example.

When your drive-thru coffee is $2.50, and you tell the barista to keep the change from your $5 bill, that might not feel significant to you, but it represents a 100 percent tip for her! Imagine the appreciation she might feel from your gesture. Give some thought to your community and the people who have served you in various ways. Do something thoughtful.

And assume the thought *always* counts.

Ideas to Spark, Connect & Create this week:

- The next time you are in a situation that suggests you give a tip, what are you going to do? (Unsolicited advice: think generously.)
- If you have children or grandchildren, take the time to explain to them what tipping is. Teach them why we tip and share your tipping philosophy with them. This is a lesson they will likely take with them for the rest of their lives.

Notes and Thoughts

CHAPTER 51

YOUR BUCKET LIST

As I sit here in my office, landscapers are outside pulling summer pansies out of the ground and replacing them with hearty orange and yellow mums. I officially traded in my flip-flops this week for cowboy boots and jeans, and the heat just kicked on in my building because it's only fifty degrees outside.

Fall has officially arrived in Massachusetts.

With the change in the season, I found myself getting reflective. I started thinking more and more about impact, the way we treat other people, and the word **legacy**.

Our community recently lost an amazing woman. She was just shy of her eighty-ninth birthday when she passed away. She and her husband had been married for seventy years. She was a leader, a philanthropist, and a mentor to many. In reading her obituary, I thought, *What a life well-lived*! It seemed like she had really done it all in her time on earth and left such a lasting legacy behind.

Days later, I read about the passing of Ruth Bader Ginsberg. Talk about a woman who made an impact. When you scroll through the list of Ginsberg's accomplishments, she seemed to have filled every moment of her eighty-seven years, creating an extraordinary legacy. Regardless of your politics, I think her story is inspiring and beyond impressive to us all.

I wonder if these two women had a bucket list. Did they intentionally set out to accomplish all the amazing things they ultimately did in their lifetimes? Did they check each one of those accomplishments off their list when they were complete?

My grandmother (Gramma Jam) had many things on her bucket list, and she was very open to sharing her list with us. Gramma Jam wanted to...

1. Learn to drive (when my grandfather passed away, she needed to get her license)
2. Learn to swim (which she eventually did in our pool, with all the grandkids cheering on and encouraging her)
3. Take a trip to Hawaii (which she took with her BFF, Mrs. Taylor)
4. Ride in a hot air balloon (which was the last item on her list, and she did that too)

Gramma Jam started tackling these items in her fifties and finished them up in her early seventies before she passed away. They were accomplished with the help and encouragement of friends and family. By the time she passed away, Gramma Jam had checked everything off her bucket list.

I love the bucket list concept. I often encourage clients to take time to get clear about the things they want to do, see, and accomplish in their lifetime—and then help them get to work on creating a plan to make those things come to fruition.

Last year we challenged our clients to choose something from their bucket lists and make it happen. Here are some of the results:

- A retired couple renovated an Airstream and are traveling cross-country to visit places they've always wanted to see.
- A local business owner transformed her backyard into a spectacular garden this year, growing all her own vegetables, and has mastered canning and pickling—while also successfully keeping her business afloat.
- An eighty-two-year-old client learned to speak Italian by taking online courses and is going to finally see the Vatican in the spring.
- A friend's son decided he didn't want to go to college this fall but instead wanted to become

a farmer. He was totally serious. So the family packed up and moved to the Midwest to support their son's dream. They cashed in his college account to put a down payment on forty acres of land, and the whole family now plays a role in running the family farm. How incredible is that?

Take a moment to think about your bucket list and your legacy. This is the time to share your wishes with others and get into action.

And from the Notorious RBG: "If you want to be a true professional, you will do something outside yourself, something to repair tears in your community, something to make life a little better for people less fortunate than you."[9]

What a message!

I encourage you to focus on your legacy, think about your community and the people you love, and look for opportunities to make a difference every single day while you still can.

Ideas to Spark, Connect & Create this week:

- What is your legacy? What are you doing now that will leave a lasting impact later? What do you want people to remember about you?
- What's on your bucket list? Does anyone know about this?

- Is there something that once was on your bucket list but you've since given up on it? What would it take to resurrect that dream and commit to making it happen? Is there someone who could help you make it come to life?
- Is there an elderly person you know who may have a bucket list item you could help them achieve? What if this week you reached out and opened the conversation with them?

Notes and Thoughts

CHAPTER 52

A LEGACY OF LOVE

I have a clear memory of being woken up early in the morning. I think I was five. It was dark out, and my sister and I were in our pajamas. We had to get into the Volkswagen Beetle (The Bug) so my parents could deliver newspapers in our neighborhood before sunrise.

Delivering newspapers was a second job my folks took on to make ends meet while Dad was trying to get his company started. As a small child, I remember us having one car. Mom helped Dad get the papers delivered before he had to go to his regular job.

On weekday mornings, we shuffled from our beds to the backseat of The Bug, laid down with our blankets and stuffed animals (no seatbelts back then), and drove up and down the streets making sure neighbors' newspapers were in their mailboxes or on their porches before they awoke. Once the papers were delivered, we then drove Dad to work so Mom could have The Bug to get us to school.

I don't know how long their two-job gig lasted or for how many years they managed a family of four with one car. I just know they worked extra hard in those early years.

As Dad's electroplating business started to become successful, he was able to give up the newspaper delivery job. He still worked overtime, however, at his company on Saturdays. My sister and I often went with him. It was a total treat.

We'd sit at the secretaries' desks, scroll blank sheets of paper into their electric typewriters, and pretend we were at work. We'd create our own invoices and memos. Sometimes Nicki would go outside to the front entrance, ring the doorbell, and I'd greet her as if she were my customer. She'd wait in the lobby for her appointment, help herself to candies from the candy jar, and eventually, I'd slide the window open behind my desk and call her in for her meeting. We'd do this for hours until Dad's Saturday work was done.

As the years went on, we upgraded from one car to two and eventually from used to new. I remember the day we took delivery of our brand-new Buick LeSabre. It was plush and fancy. My dad was so proud as he drove our family off the lot and brought it home.

My parents did life right. They started with nothing. They worked hard, and they created a vision for what their future could look like.

Over time, Dad's company grew into something special. No matter what his workday entailed, he was home every single night for dinner.

Important business lessons were often taught to us at the dinner table:

- Never spend more than you make.
- Take good care of your employees, and they will always take good care of you.
- It's not easy to be the boss, but it comes with great rewards if you choose to do the right thing for others.
- Plan for the future, but also enjoy life today.

So much of who I am, how I think, and what I now teach to others comes from my father.

I've been reflecting on my dad's legacy. Dad worked hard and did whatever it took to be a provider for our family (not just for the four of us, but for the extended family as well, although most people never knew about his quiet generosity). He built an incredible business, loved my mom like crazy, saved for our future, kept us grounded, paid for our college educations, taught me about the stock market, and took pride in how perfectly he mowed his lawn every week.

And at age fifty, my dad suffered a massive heart attack and died unexpectedly.

He never made it to retirement.

He never got to meet his future grandchildren. He never got to reap the rewards of his hard work nor celebrate all his accomplishments with my mom in their golden years.

For a long time, my father's story didn't make sense to me. The ending was all wrong.

It has taken me a long time to understand and make peace with my dad's death, especially the fact that he was only fifty years old when he passed.

Time and maturity have taught me that my dad's work may have been complete.

What he accomplished in his short lifetime was impressive—as an entrepreneur, a family man, a father, a boss, and a husband. Dad provided for us three girls, making sure we were all educated and that we were each on our way to building our own careers. I was a brand-new financial advisor, my sister was building her personal training business, and my mother was building her clientele as a new hairdresser. Ironically, we all ended up becoming self-employed entrepreneurs.

For years I have wondered, What if my father's life's work was to make sure his wife and two daughters were launched in their careers, and his own business was built to succeed without him?

For many people, that would have been considered a full life.

I share this personal story with you as a reminder that none of us know how much time we have **to get our**

own life's work done. For some, it might be measured in twice as many years as my father had.

The challenge is that we just don't know how much time we have.

Whatever our fate may be, let us learn and share **whatever we can while we can**.

Regardless of the number of years our life is measured in, let us all strive for a life well-lived.

You are now ready for your final assignment:

Ask yourself: What is your twelve-month vision for your life?

Grab a piece of paper or your journal or the blank pages offered right here, and get ready to brainstorm.

Here is the assignment: You are going to write yourself a letter. Date the letter **twelve months from today**.

Begin writing to yourself about all your accomplishments one year from now *as if they already happened*. Add as much detail as possible to create a vivid and inspiring story about how your year ended up turning out.

You will want to describe each event in the past tense: In February, the whole family went on a cruise to Alaska! I have never seen so many moose in one location. The trip was incredible and fulfilled a bucket list item for my grandmother! (Even though that experience would not have happened **yet**, you are describing it as if it has.)

As you think about each month of the upcoming year, write about what you have achieved. Include business, personal, health, and relationship breakthroughs. Describe what your family has accomplished, both personally and professionally. And last, include your hopes for the upcoming year—all of it written in the past tense, as though it already happened.

Include stretch goals, even if you have no idea how to accomplish them yet. You don't have to know how to make them happen, just that you know you want them to become a reality within the next year.

Imagine your goal for the next twelve months is to grow your business while also dedicating more time to your family. Your twelve-month vision might start with something like this:

I was thrilled that our search for an executive assistant led us to Sherry. She joined our team in June and made such an impact in a short time. By year-end, she revamped all our processes, set up workflows, and completely took over my email inbox. That freed me up to spend more time mentoring and coaching Jim, the new associate who joined us in July. In only six months, Jim has already helped grow revenue by 10 percent! The team is really coming together. I finally felt confident to leave the office for an extended vacation. My wife and I booked the ten-day trip to Disney we had been promising the kids, and we were able to spend Thanksgiving in the Magic Kingdom. I completely unplugged from emails and voicemails and had a true vacation. My wife was so happy to see me relaxed the whole week. The kids had so much fun. This year turned out to be something I'm proud of, personally and professionally.

As you write, do not edit, and do not judge.

Do not worry about figuring out the details of how these accomplishments are going to happen. Just write them all down as if they already have.

Be sure to include other important people in your twelve-month vision: expand your thoughts to include friends, family, and activities you want to invest more time in throughout the next twelve months. Write down all the confetti moments you want to create!

Most importantly, do not play this safe. This is a vision for your future—choose one that is worth celebrating.

Here's where it all begins:

FINAL THOUGHTS

Now that you've reached the end of *Confetti Moments,* I hope you've been able to engage in new conversations, enjoy deeper connections with others, celebrate the ordinary, and experience the kinds of confetti moments I promised at the beginning of this book.

Each of these fifty-two stories means something special to me. It is a privilege I get to share them with you in this collection.

As you continue on your journey, my wish is that you become even more aware of **the significance of your own life**. Continue making the most out of the time you have on earth. Have fun. Be coachable. Tip generously. Don't be afraid to integrate all the things you love into each of your days until you find that integration sweet spot. And if you need a little YOLO encouragement, this is your reminder to buy the damn truck.

When you do get to pause and appreciate those ordinary moments in life—either by yourself or shared with someone you love—please picture me in the background, tossing the confetti in celebration with you.

ACKNOWLEDGMENTS

To Kim, Charlie, Jane, Mom, Nicki, and Dave: Thank you for allowing me to showcase you and your life experiences as the subject of many of these stories. It is *from you* that I have learned the best lessons in life. And it is *because of you* that I can laugh at myself through these humbling and often hilarious vignettes. Your support means the world to me. Here's to a lifetime of confetti moments together. Love you, mean it.

To my uncle, Austin Kenefick: You are one of the smartest and most thoughtful people I know. Thank you for carefully reading through each of these chapters and editing with skill and grace. There is no doubt that your feedback made this a better book. I love how your writing has contributed so much to others over your ninety years on earth. And I can think of no one better to share our October 3 birthday with. (And yes, I ended that sentence on a preposition.)

To Auntie Mo: Thank you for your patience and generosity. I appreciate that you know me so well. I will say it one last time: **You were right**. Your creative genius helped spark the right title as well as a brilliant book cover, bringing these stories together in the most perfect package. Thank you, Babycakes.

To my Crafterday buddy, BB: Thanks for being willing to sit for hours and hours listening to '80s jams, and never getting tired of gluing and painting and cutting out paper hearts. You brought the glitter to our home—*literally*! Love, AA.

To Auntie Bev: Thanks for being such a loyal reader of my *Wednesday Wisdom* blog and for becoming such a special part of my life in recent years. You better believe that the sequel to this book is going to include a story about you. And it will be titled "I Am, I Said."

To my grandmothers, Gramma Jam & Granny Ruthie: Thank you for the memories you created for us in our childhood. It is because of you that these old stories still exist and **still matter**.

To my clients: I coined the expression "confetti moments" because of you. These two simple words sum up the milestones and celebrations you have shared with me over the past twenty-five years. **Your stories brought *Confetti Moments* to life**. Thank you for your trust and confidence. Being part of your families' journeys has been an honor and a privilege, and I can't wait to see what's ahead. For all that you have collectively accomplished, cue the confetti!

To my loyal *Wednesday Wisdom* blog readers: Thank you for two years of encouragement and for sharing your personal stories in response to mine. Every time I wondered, "Is anyone reading my *Wednesday Wisdom* emails?" I'd get a response from one of you validating that week's message. You emphatically told me that my words mattered to you. And to those of you who boldly suggested that my *Wednesday Wisdom* emails should be packaged into a book, well, that turned out to be a very good idea. **I will never forget that this project started with you**.

To my TJG family (Jessica, Jess, Angela, Jay, Caro, and Bailey): Not everyone gets to live a fully integrated life and incorporate all the elements they love into both work and home. Because of you, I experience this every day. Thank you for embracing my entrepreneurial craziness. Thanks for supporting all my new ideas (every week, in just about every meeting, including all my tangents) and for being gracious when I swiftly move on to other ideas. I love what we have built for our clients and for each other. Your consistency allows me to sneak out occasionally and write a book. **You rock.**

To the wise and brave people who have coached me over the years, specifically Paul Steffen, Pete Greider, Tim Mulroy, Jeff Photiades, Anne Weiss, Jessica Holloway, Brendan Naughton, and Brad Somma: Thank you for believing in me and nudging me before I was ready to grow. Thank you for knowing when to push me forward and also for knowing when to reign me in. Your collective wisdom, tough questions, and unwavering patience helped get me to where I am right now. Please know that in moments of big decisions, I still hear your guiding voices in my head. You have made a permanent mark on my head and my heart. Thank you for teaching me what it means to be coachable.

To the kick-ass women of Coalition (with a special shout-out to Michelle Pedigo & Joe Sparacio for being our Champions): It is my greatest honor to be your coach. I want you to know that working with you all is a career highlight for me. Thank you for letting me into your world. I appreciate each of you individually, and I love even more the power within our group. Cue the confetti for the sisterhood that we are building together. And know that we have only just begun!

To my Strategic Coach Community (notably Dan Sullivan, Kristi Chambers, Shannon Waller, Julia Waller, Marilyn Waller, Kary Oberbrunner, Will Duke, John Stichter, and Carolyn Nolan): Thank you for your brilliant ideas, intelligent shortcuts, and life-changing conversations over the past four years. When I met you, I shared that I wanted to spend my days teaching clients, coaching financial advisors, and writing a best-selling book, but I had no idea where to begin. Little did I know that it would begin in October 2018, in Toronto, with all of you. Thank you for being my WHOs.

And lastly, to my twenty-one-year-old self during senior year at Middlebury College: If I could go back and give you advice, it would be this: Keep writing. Keep tracking your goals. Keep your vision clear. Most of all, be patient. It is going to take a long time to publish your book. You're going to have to do a lot of work first— for about thirty years—before it all comes together. Your career as a financial advisor will be fulfilling and wonderful—and will ultimately bring you back to your writing. Pay close attention to the details and appreciate the journey because it's going to be filled with confetti-worthy moments.

END NOTES

1 McKeown, Greg. *Essentialism: The Disciplined Pursuit of Less.* New York: Crown, 2020.

2 ibid.

3 Santora, Marc and Vivian Yee. "In Suez Canal, Tides Rise and Fall, Salvagers Toil, but Ship Remains Stuck." *The New York Times.* March 28, 2021. https://www.nytimes.com/live/2021/03/28/world/suez-canal-stuck-ship.

4 Walsh, Regan. *Heart Boss: Trust Your Gut, Shed Your Shoulds, and Create a Life You Love.* Houndstooth Press, 2021.

5 Kwai, Isabella. "'You Could Compare It to a Picasso': Pigeon Sells for $1.9 Million." *The New York Times.* November 16, 2020.

6 Reuters. "Fact check: Tomb of the unknown Soldier sentinels must observe rigorous protocols, but can still drink alcohol off duty, swear in public." May 26, 2020. https://www.reuters.com/article/uk-factcheck-tomb-unknown-soldier/fact-check-tomb-of-the-unknown-soldier-sentinels-must-observe-rigorous-protocols-but-can-still-drink-alcohol-off-duty-swear-in-public-idUSKBN2322DK

7 Paulson, Dave. "Chris Young and Kane Brown on 'Famous Friends,' CMA Nominations: 'A Full Circle.'" *The Tennessean,* September 29, 2021. https://www.tennessean.com/story/

entertainment/music/2021/09/29/chris-young-kane-brown-interview-famous-friends-cma-nominations/5915997001/.

8   Adele. "Adele: One Night Only." *CBS*. November 14, 2021.

9   Clifford, Catherine. "Ruth Bader Ginsburg Says This Is the Secret to Living a Meaningful Life." *CNBC.com*. https://www.cnbc.com/2017/02/07/ruth-bader-ginsburg-says-this-is-the-secret-to-a-meaningful-life.html.

ABOUT THE AUTHOR

Amy Jamrog is an author, coach, keynote speaker, CEO of The Jamrog Group, and the founder of Four Wings Consulting. Throughout her twenty-five-year career in financial services, Amy has helped hundreds of families successfully navigate money conversations, create new possibilities, and take action toward their dreams. While equipping her clients to succeed, Amy also sought to share her ideas with other financial advisors in the hopes of making their lives easier and their work more fun. Through Four Wings Consulting, Amy offers a wealth of financial planning and coaching ideas, as well as tools and solutions, to help financial advisors better serve their clients and lead their teams more effectively.

Beyond coaching and financial planning, Amy offers keynote presentations designed to educate anyone looking to create more confetti moments in their lives.

To learn more about working with Amy and her team on your financial plan, please visit www.jamrog.group. For advisors who want to learn about Amy's coaching and keynote presentations, please visit www.fourwings.consulting. And for anyone wanting more confetti moments, visit www.confettimoments.com

ethos
collective

Are You
Confetti
Ready?

TAKE THE ASSESSMENT TO
DISCOVER YOUR CONFETTI
READINESS SCORE™

confettimoments.com/assessment

Cue the Confetti!

CHECK OUT AMY'S BLOG FOR INSIGHTFUL PERSONAL STORIES AND OTHER CONFETTI MOMENTS YOU'LL LOVE.

confettimoments.com/ cue-the-confetti

Connect with Amy

 FACEBOOK.COM/AMYQJAMROG

 @AMYJAMROG

 CONFETTIMOMENTS.COM

Join the Confetti movement!
Use #confettimoments to share what
matters.

Keynote Speaker

WOULD YOUR ORGANIZATION BENEFIT FROM MORE CONFETTI MOMENTS?

Invite Amy to speak at your next event!

www.confettimoments.com

THE JAMROG GROUP

Financial planning for happy people seeking clarity, simplification, and organization of their lives.

Connect with Us

Scan the QR code or visit us at the links below.

Website: www.jamrog.group
Facebook: www.facebook.com/jamroggroup
LinkedIn: www.linkedin.com/company/thejamroggroup

BLOCKCHAIN
VERIFIED IP™

Powered by Easy IP™

Made in United States
North Haven, CT
18 August 2023

40477139R00191